Small Boat,
Wide Sea
PARENTING
IN THE 21ST CENTURY

Small Boat, Wide Sea

PARENTING
IN THE 21ST CENTURY

J. ANN MUMFORD, PH.D.

Cover photograph: Bart Larson
www.reflectionsofglory.com

Cover design: Brenton Mumford
www.brentonmumford.com

Scripture quotations marked (KJV) are taken from
The Holy Bible, King James Version, Cambridge, 1769.
Scripture quotations marked (NIV) are taken from
The Holy Bible, New International Version®. NIV®.
Copyright © 1973, 1978, 1984, by International
Bible Society. Used by permission of Zondervan.
Scripture quotations marked (MSG) are taken
from *The Message* by Eugene Peterson, copyright ©
1993, 1994, 1995, 1996, 2000, 2001, 2002. Used by
permission of NavPress publishing group. All rights
reserved.

ISBN 0-9755001-1-2

Published by Kingsgate Publishing
1000 Pannell Street, Suite A, Columbia, MO 65201
sales@kingsgatepublishing.com
www.kingsgatepublishing.com

Acknowledgements

Thank you to the many parents who stimulated
my thinking, shaped my perspective
and compelled me to search for answers.

Thank you to my family and friends
who believed I had something worthwhile to say
and prodded me to put my thoughts in writing.

Thank you to Ranelle, Bette and Earl
who provided invaluable feedback in the book's final stages.

Thank you to my son Brenton,
whose assistance, support and encouragement
allowed a dream to become reality.

JAM

With gratitude …

To my mother, Edith Gutwein,
who epitomizes a caring, accepting, and loving parent.

To my husband and best friend, Eric,
with whom I've shared the exciting parenting journey.

To our older son, Rick, whose birth unleashed
a flood of indescribable maternal love .

To our younger son, Brenton, whose unique perspective of life
has blessed me immeasurably.

To God, my Heavenly Father, in whose love and care I flourish
and on whom I depend for life itself.

Contents

Preface

Any successful voyage requires thoughtful preparation, pragmatic planning, and unexpected adaptations along the way. The parenting journey is no exception. But no two families can, or should, follow exactly the same path. Family dynamics, individual traits, genetic influences and belief systems all have an impact on our attitudes, choices and behaviors. As parents, we have the responsibility and privilege of thoughtfully plotting a course that best suits our family's collective and individual needs.

Small Boat, Wide Sea is designed to assist parents in promoting optimal development during the early years and laying a solid foundation for wise choices during adolescence. You are invited to thoughtfully, realistically, expectantly and confidently chart your family's course through the unexplored waters that lie ahead.

One

What a seemingly overwhelming task to put pen to paper (figuratively, if not literally) and attempt to write a book on parenting! Hundreds of books—some with catchy titles, some that zero in on the challenges of particular stages and phases, and others that present "formulas" for parenting success—are already in print. Books on bonding, discipline, and self-esteem are but a click of the mouse or a drive to the local mall away. An undertaking such as this necessitates an honest appraisal of the task at hand and a humble evaluation of one's credentials. What, if anything, has been left unsaid? Who, if anyone, is qualified to address such a difficult and critical topic?

Parenting, like any aspect of behavioral sciences, is as complex as human nature itself. Just as a nightshirt's claim of "one size fits all" is called into question by my size 2 petite frame, only the inexperienced or naïve would recommend a predetermined, formula-type approach to raising children. No matter how sound parenting advice might appear on the surface, to be effective it must be fitted not only to each family's, but each child's, unique characteristics and needs.

Strangely enough, this book regarding parenting during early childhood was primarily motivated by my fascination and concern with *adolescent* behaviors, such as reckless driving, marijuana smoking, and binge drinking. Attempting to counsel and console battle-weary parents led me to an impassioned search for answers to an age-old question: "Why do such smart kids make such dumb choices?" Through the years, I have listened carefully to both parents' and children's perspectives of the causes and consequences of risk-taking behaviors. The intention of this book is to share my insights with those of you who are currently preparing your children (and yourself) for the stage of adolescence that lies just around the corner. Hopefully you will be encouraged to consider, plan, and embrace the journey of parenting on which you've embarked.

As a daughter, sister, wife, mother and grandmother, I have experienced first-hand the joys and challenges of relationships within the family. As a friend, I have been both the recipient and the provider of parenting counsel. As a speaker, I have stood before many groups of parents who were seeking to understand temperamental and developmental issues and translate them into effective practice. As a professor, I have learned a great deal from my students and attempted to impart credible parenting ideologies to them, tomorrow's child psychologists, journalists, social workers, and—most importantly—parents. As a researcher, I have been involved in lengthy one-on-one conversations with adolescents whose lives have been irreversibly altered by poor choices. In a diverse array of roles, I have observed, examined, and contemplated child behaviors and parenting practices, attempting to make some sense of possible correlations and connections.

My own personal experience has absolutely convinced me that parenting is one of life's greatest blessings. I am equally certain that it is not for the weak of heart. I will endeavor to present a balanced, realistic view of parenting's challenges and rewards and some practical suggestions. My desire is to motivate, support, and encourage you, rather than offer you a ready-made map, as you chart the course for your own family. My prayer is that the suggestions in this book will elicit a desire in you to chart your own individualized and gratifying course through the wide sea of parenting.

My pledge to you, the reader, is to not trivialize the potential trauma of your 3-year-old giving herself a haircut or your 7-year-old routinely swapping his nutritional lunch for two candy bars and a baseball card. I will validate your feelings and I will be honest about my own struggles as a parent. Although this book is based on empirical research, with references listed in the bibliography, I am assuming that you are not interested in or impressed by jargon-laden, technical descriptions of complex theories of human development. I will provide only enough explanation to lend credibility to the "bottom line"—the application to your parenting. A further assumption is that you have limited time for reading much other than Dr. Seuss books and the instructions on children's aspirin labels. Therefore, I am committed to brevity.

Because adolescents themselves have taught me so much, excerpts of their stories are interspersed throughout the pages of this book. As you read, you will see the names Tonya, Sara, George, Ali, Rebecca, Bob, Jack, Faith, Mike, Opie, Liz, Steve and Mindy (all pseudonyms), who engaged in potentially harmful behaviors and subsequently spent a portion of their teen years in a residential treatment center. They openly shared their stories so that others could better understand why children sometimes choose to walk a path that results in pain for themselves and others. I am deeply indebted to each of them.

My hope is that every parent who picks up this book will find some tip, insight, or suggestion that will be meaningful and useful. But I am very much aware that a number of circumstances that greatly complicate parenting are not addressed. I do not deal specifically with topics such as parenting children with special needs, single or step-parenting, raising children in poverty, or being part of a minority culture. These matters have been left to others who are much better qualified than I to address them.

Finally, you will find a common thread throughout the pages of this book: references to the Bible and the importance of a connection with Someone greater than oneself. This reflects my belief in a God who lovingly and wisely guides us through life's waters, be they peaceful or troubled.

Two
SMALL BOAT, WIDE SEA

Dear Lord, be good to me.
The sea is so wide and my boat is so small.

- Irish Fisherman's Prayer -

"No one ever said it would be easy." I don't know the origin of this phrase; I can only speculate that it was first uttered by a person in the midst of parenting. When new parents and their "precious bundle" leave the maternity ward of the local hospital, arms loaded with congratulatory balloons, flowers, and baby booties, they are catapulted into the world of parenting, ready or not. Some have had no training or experience at all, some have taken an 8-week course in which they've practiced changing a baby doll or teddy bear's diaper, and others have cared for younger siblings and read dozens of parenting books. However, even the most prepared can find themselves insecure and overwhelmed. I assure you, I speak from personal experience.

Having been married to my childhood sweetheart for three years, I was ecstatic when I learned we were expecting our first child. My husband had just completed college and had his first "real" job. I eagerly and happily exchanged any professional aspirations to realize my true heart's desire— becoming a mother. In the midst of what has been called the image-making stage[1] in which one idealizes parenting, my life truly was a dream. With no regrets, I quit my job early in the pregnancy because of all-day "morning sickness." I carried our son, during a long hot summer, two and half weeks past the predicted due date. Nevertheless, my pregnancy was filled with excited anticipation. On a very limited budget, we set up a nursery: a hand-me-down crib; a stack of cloth diapers; six tiny gowns with drawstring bottoms; a small sewing rocker and an oak dresser purchased at a second-hand furniture store.

Having studied child development and read numerous parenting books and magazines, our hearts as well as our home were ready for the arrival of our first child. But along with the labor pains came a rude awakening. The birthing process itself was long and difficult and, as a result of complications from anesthesia during the delivery, baby Ricky and I remained in the hospital for ten days. The immediate mother-child bonding, which many child development experts claim is imperative for optimum child outcomes, was greatly hampered by my inability to care for our infant. Once, when my own pain made it impossible for me to feed him, the nurse accused me of not wanting to be a mother. The heart-break I felt at that moment still brings tears to my eyes, more than 35 years later. My dreams were being crushed and my maternal self-worth was rapidly diminishing.

Back at our small, two-bedroom apartment, physical and emotional exhaustion and sleep deprivation continued to take their toll. Although generally healthy, our tiny son was discontent and seldom slept for more than an hour at a time. My husband was incredibly loving and supportive, but he was gone each day from 7:00 a.m. until 5:30 p.m. and required at least some sleep at night. So I struggled through the long days and longer nights smiling on the outside, at least in the presence of others, but crying on the inside. I vividly remember dressing Ricky in an adorable blue and white sailor's suit with a matching hat and propping him in the corner of the sofa. When a friend admired him, my first thought was that maybe I should give him to her. I was certain that she would be a better mother than I. Thus, with initial joyful expectations dissolving into near hopelessness, my parenting journey began.

Why, in a book whose goal is to support and encourage parents, would I begin by sharing some of my most difficult struggles? First, I want you to know that I understand the pain of feeling like a less-than-perfect parent. Second, from my current vantage point, my experience of years of parenting clearly demonstrates how times of joy can over-shadow—even totally eclipse—the times of difficulty. In spite of my early misgivings and other bumps along the way, I cannot imagine anyone feeling more fortunate to be a mother. Third, I believe it is more common than we are prone to admit for parents to feel as if they are navigating a very wide sea in a very small boat. Parents need to know that feeling stymied, incompetent, and alone is relatively commonplace and is nothing of which to be ashamed. Finally, and most importantly, just as surely as I can admit inadequacies and challenges as a parent, I can point to One who has always provided the strength and direction I need. I have relied heavily on Scriptural promises such as "Those who hope in the Lord will renew their strength" [2] and "If any of you lacks wisdom, he should ask God, who gives generously . . ."[3] Much as sailors can look to the North Star as a consistently accurate compass, we can trust Him to guide our tiny, turmoil-prone boats.

Three
CHARTING THE COURSE

Knowing your purpose gives your life meaning,
simplicity, focus and motivation.
It also prepares you for eternity.

- Rick Warren[1]

We love our children so, of course, we have high hopes for them. We hope they will maximize their God-given aptitudes and minimize their seeming deficiencies. We hope they will make wise choices regarding relationships, educational opportunities, and careers. I remember that, as a preschooler, one of our sons decided he wanted to be a garbage collector. I encouraged him to keep his options open.

As we envision our young children growing up to be all they can be, we must remind ourselves that dreams do not magically turn into reality. Perhaps this reality is what Plutarch had in mind when he so eloquently stated, "No man ever wetted clay and then left it, as if there would be bricks by chance and fortune." Likewise, when a man and woman conceive a child, how foolish to assume that a life of meaning and purpose will automatically unfold! But many of the parents of the more than four million babies born in our country each year have no map, no compass, no specific destination, and little comprehension of the rigors of the journey ahead.

It's not as if any of us would intentionally leave our children's future to chance. But sometimes the immediacy of the moment—runny noses, messy diapers, untied shoes—robs us of sufficient time and energy to reflect on the impact of our daily actions and decisions on the adult our child will one day become. How do we ensure that our children's lives don't get lost in the shuffle of living?

When we see an SUV bumper sticker announcing that there's "precious cargo on board," we can assume the cargo is a very tiny person strapped into a disproportionately large, well-padded car seat. Completely dependent on the big person behind the steering wheel in the front seat, the child has no concerns about the trip or the destination. But can our children look to us just as confidently when it comes to the challenging journey of life? Are they safely strapped in and confident that there's someone older and wiser behind the wheel?

Goal-Setting

When it comes to goal-setting, a well-worn adage comes to mind. The phrase "If you aim at nothing you'll hit it" can be aptly applied to parenting. We need a target, a goal, a sense of direction for ourselves as well as for our children. As Thomas Carlyle stated, "The man without a purpose is like a ship without a rudder—a waif, a nothing, no man."

Sure, we all have some general goals for our children, an idea of what we want them to do and be. We want them to be happy and healthy. But how can we, with our very human ideals and perspective, look beyond the obvious and align our goals for our children with God's purposes for each of us? Let me share with you a Bible verse that helped me organize my thoughts and served as a model for my hopes, plans, and daily prayers for our sons. "…Jesus grew in wisdom and stature, and in favor with God and man."[2] This verse encompasses the intellectual, physical, spiritual, and social-emotional development of the perfect God-man and provides us with a structure for considering our hopes and dreams for our children.

I have used the Luke 2:52 model as a prayer guide since our sons were infants. I prayed daily that they would mature in wisdom, stature, favor with God, and favor with man. I elaborated on each of these areas, adapting my prayers to the persons, situations, challenges, needs, and opportunities in their lives at that time.

Needless to say, as our sons grew and changed, so did my prayers. My prayers that a 3-year-old would understand what it means to love Jesus eventually became prayers that a 13-year-old would understand what it means for Jesus to love him. My prayers that a 6-year-old's T-ball injuries would heal quickly were changed to prayers that a 16-year-old's driving would result in no injuries. My prayers that a 2-year-old wouldn't bite his best friend were replaced by prayers that a 12-year-old would choose his best friend wisely.

Not only did my aspirations for our children give direction to my prayers, but my prayers, in turn, shaped my aspirations. As I prayed each day that our sons would "love Jesus more than anyone or anything else," I considered whether there were indications of maturation in this area. I also contemplated the effectiveness with which I was fulfilling my parental role by instilling and modeling a belief system to guide their thoughts and actions throughout their lives.

My prayers reflected not only my passionate desire to see our sons grow as Jesus did but also my feelings of inadequacy as a parent. I continually asked for God's strength, wisdom, and direction and prayed that *my* plans for my children would be consistent with *His* plans for them. It became very evident that goal-setting not only provided direction for my children; it also served to challenge and refine me.

Parental Role Modeling

Think for a moment about these words of Francis of Assisi: "Preach always, but if necessary use words."[3] The Apostle Paul also emphasized actions, not words, when he wrote, "Be imitators of God . . . and live a life of love"[4] Do we want our children to be Christ-like? If so, *we* must imitate Him, because, whether we like it or not, our children will imitate us. Think for a moment about the ways in which you emulate your own parents—perhaps your penchant for peanut butter and banana sandwiches, your passion for the down-trodden or your political convictions. After all is said and done, much of charting the course for our children is dependent on our leading the way by *modeling* the attitudes and behaviors we want them to exhibit.

As a simplistic example, if a goal for my young child is that he learn to respect authority and follow rules, I probably shouldn't grab his tiny hand and rush him across the street while the "no walking" sign is blinking. Explaining to him that it is "okay" because no cars were coming is pointless; situational ethics are far beyond his level of cognitive functioning. My husband actually learned this lesson through experience, as he recalls that our son would resolutely stand on the curb until the "walk" icon appeared, despite his father's coaxing to proceed. Although children's development is a gradual, long-term process, it is formed by seemingly insignificant daily behaviors and decisions, which can set precedents, serve as examples, and lead to consequences that will ultimately shape their future.

* * * * *

The following questions may be helpful as we contemplate what our children are observing in us:

- Do my children hear me speak in words and tones that I want them to imitate?

- Do I model behaviors consistent with what I expect and desire from my children?
- Do my words and actions impart a consistent message?
- If my children were to use five adjectives to describe me, what would those adjectives be? How do they compare with the adjectives I hope will describe them when they are adults?

* * * * *

Moses, the God-appointed leader of the Israelites, certainly understood the importance of parental role-modeling. He had seen a generation of people make a series of terrible mistakes by questioning, doubting and betraying their God. As a result, all of his generation eventually died in the barren wilderness rather than enjoying the lush Promised Land. In Deuteronomy 6, Moses is grooming the next generation and undoubtedly hoping for much better results. As he commands them to "Love the Lord your God with all your heart and with all your soul and with all your strength," he speaks about the importance of their having a personal belief, telling them the commandments should be "on [their] hearts."[5] Then he strongly emphasizes passing their beliefs on to their children: "Impress [these commandments] on your children. Talk about them when you sit at home and when you walk along the road, when you lie down and when you get up. Tie them as symbols on your hands and bind them on your foreheads. Write them on the doorframes of your houses and on your gates."[6] Tying the commandments on their hands symbolized God's control over their behaviors; binding them on their foreheads represented God's control over their thoughts, and writing them on the doorframes of their houses and gates proclaimed their beliefs to all. Godly living was obviously not meant to be a once-a-week ritual, but rather an everyday way of life.

I am also reminded of another Biblical model, Joshua, who provides a great example of determining (and publicly declaring) his intentions. As leader of the Israelites, he strongly exhorts them to "fear the Lord and serve Him with all faithfulness."[7] But he quickly acknowledges that each person must make his or her own choice, as he adds, "But if serving the Lord seems undesirable to you, then choose for yourselves this day whom you will serve."[8]

Joshua then speaks definitively on behalf of the entity for whom he is ultimately responsible, his own family. "As for me and my household, *we* will serve the Lord,"[9] he proclaims. Although it's simple to *say* that we have decided to "serve the Lord," in reality our daily choices are the true indicator of which gods we have chosen—not only for ourselves, but for our family as well. Decisions regarding the people with whom we associate, the influences to which we are exposed, the activities in which we are involved and the responsibilities we assume all give direction to the course of our lives.

Staying on Course

One of the best incentives for steadily steering our children toward thoughtfully planned, predetermined goals is a consciousness of the critical importance of the task at hand. Perhaps you are familiar with the work of researcher Judith Harris, who raised eyebrows not only in the world of academia but in society at large in the 1990s when she challenged the "nurture assumption," that is, that parenting has a great influence on child outcomes. Harris' personal experience and research led her to assert that we need to stop believing that parents have crucial or long-lasting effects on their children.[10] In the *New Yorker*,[11] Harris is quoted as saying,

> A lot of people who should be contributing children to our society . . . are reluctant to do it . . . because they feel it requires such a huge commitment. If [parents] knew that it was O.K. to have a child and let it be reared by a nanny or put it in a day-care center, or even send it to a boarding school, maybe they'd believe that it would be O.K. to have a kid. You can have a kid without having to devote your entire life—your entire emotional expenditure—to this child for the next twenty years.

As you might have guessed, Harris' and my perception of parenting are quite dissimilar. In fact, if you adhere to her beliefs, you will find this book to be quite impractical and possibly even absurd. To be fair to Harris, few if any students of behavioral sciences would refute her contention that vastly differing parenting styles may lead to similar child outcomes. Further, similar parenting sometimes results in vastly different child outcomes.

However, the fact that there is no guaranteed link between child outcome and parenting style does not lead me to willingly allow someone else to usurp my role as my children's primary caregiver. Rather, given all the other potential influences, it increases my resolve to fulfill what I believe to be my responsibility as a parent: to plan for my child's future, to navigate the parenting waters with a dogged sense of determination and purpose, and to never, ever abandon ship.

Four
EMBARKING ON THE JOURNEY

From small beginnings come great things.
- American Proverb -

In my mind, a necessary component of any discussion of child development or parenting is recognizing the critical importance of children's first experiences. As providers and protectors, parents are largely responsible for what their young children see, hear, feel, touch and taste. Think for a moment about an infant's total helplessness and dependency. Does she go to sleep with background sounds of soothing music or a violent movie? Is she swathed in a soft blanket or are her tiny arms and legs left dangling and chilly? Are her wakening whimpers met with a sensitive, reassuring voice or is she ignored until her piercing cries become intolerable to her caregiver?

The significance and potential consequences of a child's early impressions, interactions, relationships and training cannot be overstated. As we set sail with our young child, what transpires in the first few furlongs sets the stage for the journey ahead.

Plato certainly understood the implications of early experiences, when he said,

The beginning is the most important part of any work, especially in the case of a young and tender thing; for that is the time at which the character is being formed and the desired impression is more readily taken. Shall we just carelessly allow children to hear any casual tales which may be devised by casual persons, and to receive ideas into their minds the very opposite of those which we would wish them to have?[1]

Although childhood educators and researchers have long recognized and acknowledged the importance of children's early experiences, over the past decade findings in the scientific world have greatly furthered our understanding of this phenomenon. We now know that a brain's "hard wiring," the connecting of the neurons, occurs during a child's first few years. Pathways in the brain, developed through either positive or negative experiences, become strong and permanent with frequent use; conversely, they become weak or even extinct with infrequent use. As an example, if a toddler's teary appeal for comfort when he skins his knees is consistently met with the admonition "Quit crying. You need to be tough!" the connection in his brain that equates demonstration of emotions with weakness will become strong. This association will eventually affect his reaction to his own, as well as insensitivity to others', physical and emotional pain. On the other hand, if a skinned knee is met by an exaggerated display of sympathy and concern, his brain will interpret any sort of physical discomfort as trauma deserving of much attention and pampering.

Related to wiring of the brain, the term "internal model" describes brain imprints that determine a child's perception of himself and others.[2] The internal working models of babies who experience an affectionate, fostering environment assure them they are lovable, acceptable, and worthy. The nurturing adults in their lives are seen as dependable and responsive to their needs. These children's early beliefs about themselves and others enable them to develop into sensitive, trusting, and respectful persons. Once again, the opposite is also true. When children are angry, fearful, and distrustful, we can surmise that their internal models have convinced them they themselves have little worth and others are not to be trusted.

In an intriguing application of brain development to early childhood development, one parenting program describes the correlation between early experiences and the functioning of various parts of the brain: the brain stem, the limbic system, and the prefrontal lobe.[3] Very young children, as well as some older children and even adults who feel physically threatened, respond to stimuli in a survival ("fight or flight") mode. Arousal and survival responses, which originate in the brain stem, typically include aggression (kicking, hitting, pushing, biting) and withdrawal. Children raised in insensitive and uncaring environments remain stuck in the brain stem mode, sometimes for life. Someone functioning at this level readily succumbs to self-centered, thoughtless, knee-jerk responses with no regard to potential consequences or others' well-being. Sadly, many adults who find themselves behind bars have never learned to respond to difficulties at a level beyond the brain stem. Conversely, children who live in a context of safety and security learn to move from brain stem responses to a higher functioning level of the brain, the limbic system.

Much as brain stem reactions are physical, the limbic system's are emotional in nature.[4] Sobbing, whining, pouting and verbal outbursts are emotional responses to sadness, perceived inequity and unfulfilled wants or needs. Validation of children's feelings, through empathy and understanding, helps them to learn the art of successfully identifying, demonstrating and controlling their emotions.

As is true of physical responses, some persons never move past emotionally volatile responses to stimuli. Although appropriately venting emotions is necessary and even therapeutic, exclusively emotionally-driven decisions and behaviors lead to undue stress, conflicts in relationships and feelings of helplessness. Beyond emotions, the next level of functioning involves the brain's frontal lobe, which is capable of consistently sound decision-making.

The frontal lobe is the area of the brain in which thinking and problem-solving occur.[5] Young children who are fighting over the same toy can be taught to take turns, thus resolving conflict without hitting (a brain stem response) or yelling

"That's not fair!" (a limbic system response). When we teach children how to react to stimuli in appropriate ways, we are encouraging the development of an invaluable tool for life: self-control, or self-regulation.

When our sons were very young, one of the songs they learned (and we all sang around the house) described self-control in very simplistic terms. "Self-control is just controlling myself/It's listening to my heart, and doing what is smart/Self-control is the very best way to go/so I think that I'll control myself."[6]

Yes, self-control really *is* the very best way to go, not only for children but for us adults as well. Remember, what we model as parents—e.g., whether we respond to life's challenges and disappointments with composure and control or with an obvious lack thereof—plays a major role in whether our children will function primarily in the brain stem, the limbic system, or the frontal lobe.

As our little ones begin the journey of life, our privilege and responsibility is to attempt to ensure that their early experiences equip them with constructive hard-wiring of the brain, affirming internal working models, and the ability to respond in an appropriate manner to various stimuli.

Five
CAMARADERIE AMONG THE CREW

*It is better to bind your children to you
by a feeling of respect, and by gentleness, than by fear.*

- Terence[1]

While other parts of this book address the issue of external influences on our family, the focus in this section is on the internal: the relationships, interactions and dynamics within the home. Much as a ship's crew must function as a team to keep the vessel on course, so the family unit must be characterized by a sense of teamwork that is dependent upon mutual cooperation and support.

Specifically, families need to function in such a way that *all* members feel unconditionally loved, respected and accepted. These factors are so intertwined that there is no obvious way to delineate them. All three seem to grow out of a sense of connectedness among family members, which I refer to here as cohesion.

Cohesion

Several years ago I developed a seminar for parents of

adolescents that I called "Parent-Adolescent Connectedness: Protection against Unacceptable Adolescent Social and Moral Behaviors." This seminar was driven by something I thought parents ought to know: research findings consistently suggest that when parents and their adolescents have warm and caring relationships, teens are less likely to engage in delinquency, violence, and substance use.[2][3]

While the above-mentioned research found that family cohesion lessened the chances that teens would engage in destructive behaviors, my own research unveiled a complementary theme: cohesion was the *missing* component in the homes of many teens, who, as a result of poor choices and strained relationships, were living at a residential facility away from their families. George, for example, said his parents never talked with each other, and described his family as a whole as "pretty much different people doing their own thing." This was remarkably similar to Sara's description of family life: "Everyone would just kind of do their own thing in a way, so it's kind of like the environment was just you'd take care of yourself." Rebecca said that when she was at home she purposely talked on the phone to avoid her parents. Bailey described her family members as individuals who didn't care and didn't listen. And, perhaps in one of the most disconcerting revelations regarding animosity toward parents, Tonya described being faced with the choice of either being arrested by the police or going home.

She chose the former, and explained in a matter-of-fact manner, "So, I was arrested and [the police] took me, because I didn't want to go with my parents."

The point is not whether the relationships in these homes were actually as strained and distant as the teens perceived or their comments would imply. Rather, we must remember that their perceptions and feelings were real to them and likely played a role in the way they distanced themselves and eventually rebelled against their parents. Although explaining human behavior is anything but an exacting art, we *can* say that as family cohesion decreases the probability that children will engage in harmful behaviors appears to increase.

When introducing this topic, I used the word "mutual" to describe the desired cooperation and support within a family. As we know, relationships are bi-directional; both parents and children contribute to the family dynamics in positive and/or negative ways. And, as they become older, children have a greater responsibility to think of others and not just themselves. We don't expect a three-year-old to come to the kitchen during meal preparation and ask if he can do anything to help. It is not unrealistic, however, to expect an eight-year-old to do so. That being said, we must remember that the duty of modeling and promoting positive qualities clearly falls on the shoulders of the parents.

Unconditional love

Unconditional love can be described as a love that we do nothing to deserve and can do nothing to destroy. Even though it may be difficult to grasp or explain, we all know that love is something for which all humans innately crave. This was evident as I talked with teens who were attempting to fill an emotional void by searching for love outside the family parameters. In Sara's words,

> My parents weren't always there . . . and I could never really tell if they loved me. I needed to go somewhere else to find that, and so all my friends were drinking and that kind of like drew me to it, just searching for something to take care of me, I guess, in a way.

Sara sensed that a critical component was missing in her relationship with her parents. The absence of unconditional love, at least in her perception, made her particularly vulnerable to peer influences.

What does it mean for parents to love their children unconditionally? I believe the following statement captures its essence: "Before becoming a mother I had a hundred theories on how to bring up children. Now I have seven children and only one theory; love them, especially when they least deserve it."[4]

We as parents don't have to be reminded to love our babies as they sleep peacefully, clinging to their teddy bears or blankets for security in our absence. We adore our three-year-olds as they emerge from their preschool classroom with their bright red "I love Daddy" backpack dangling from their tiny shoulders. We proudly sit in the bleachers as our 6-year-olds don seemingly disproportionately large batting helmets and step to the plate. We beam with pride as our 8-year-old sings in the church's Angel Choir. Loving the lovely, the adorable, the cute, or the charming isn't much of a challenge.

It is precisely at the point that effortless love stops, that supernatural (i.e., unconditional) love starts. The latter never fails, or even waivers, due to circumstances (no matter how trying) or performance (no matter how disappointing). The Bible simplistically yet eloquently describes unconditional love as "the more excellent way."[5] Love *is* patient, kind, trusting, hopeful, and persevering.[6] Love *is not* rude, self-seeking or easily angered.[7] Unconditional love is unrestricted, undeserved and absolute.

Our demonstration of love toward our children during their early years has a great impact on many aspects of their development, including their sense of worth. Accepting and valuing them, and thus promoting their self-esteem, is truly one of the best gifts we can give our children. In fact, a healthy self-esteem was a quality conspicuously and consistently absent from the troubled teens with whom I spoke. Whether their labels originated with themselves or others, I do not know. However, with few exceptions the respondents perceived themselves negatively. I sadly listened to them use terms including "dysfunctional," "bad," "the one who gets in trouble," "pretty messed up," "not good," "not typical" and "not normal" to describe themselves. Although it is difficult to specify the exact connection among a perceived absence of parental love, troubled behaviors and self-deprecating notions, a seeming link cannot be ignored.

Using the term "social mapping," one psychologist uses the following analogy to describe children's representations of themselves and their worlds: "Some children see themselves as powerful, secure countries, surrounded by allies. Others see themselves as poor little islands, surrounded by an empty ocean or hostile enemies."[8]

This concept of a child's need for love and security is poignantly illustrated by the childhood experience of a dear friend of mine. At the age of twelve, his family began to disintegrate. His mother's mental breakdown led to her being institutionalized and he and his siblings were taken to a children's home. His parents subsequently divorced and he remained in the residential facility for two years. He recalls,

> By the second year I was very unhappy and really hated the superintendent—a harsh, unloving man—and the whole experience. I was taking Spanish that year in school and combining that with my unhappiness I invented a hide-a-way world for myself called the Republica del Sabado or the Republic of Saturday. I was

the only citizen of this republic and I could escape there into my own dream world. This world was so important to me that eventually I found a small spot in the woods behind the barn where I staked out an area to provide an actual physical location for my Republic.[9]

In the absence of a home that provided a loving refuge for which all children crave, this imaginative and resourceful young teen created his own country to which he could escape.

Parental love, given freely and unconditionally, provides protection against children's foes such as low self-esteem, fear, anger, and loneliness. As parents, we strive for this degree of love, but do we ever fall short? If you'd ask me whether I have always loved my children unconditionally, I would probably somewhat indignantly reply, "Of course!" To add credibility to my definitive answer, I would admit that there have been times when I haven't *liked* our sons, but I certainly have always *loved* them. Unfortunately, if I honestly compare my thoughts and actions to the I Corinthians 13 standards of patience, kindness, trust, hope, and perseverance, it becomes all too obvious that I have failed—rather miserably, at times—to love my children as I should. *Just looking at the very first condition of absolute love— patience—is a painful reality check for me.*

Perhaps you can identify with my shortcomings on this matter. If so, rather than let missed opportunities of the past cause undue regrets and discouragement, we can learn from them and move on with determination to do better. Each day provides myriads of opportunities to love our children unconditionally.

* * * * *

As a means of assessment, let's ask ourselves these questions.

- On a scale of 1-10, how do I rate myself on each of the following I Corinthians 13 qualities as I interact with my children:
  - patient
  - kind
  - protective
  - trusting
  - hopeful
  - persevering
  - not rude
  - not self-centered
  - not easily angered

- What specific steps can I take to improve any of the above qualities I've rated 7 or lower?
- Are there certain recognizable, predictable patterns in my less than loving responses (e.g., Am I more likely to be rude when I'm rushed or preoccupied)? If so, how can I change these patterns?
- In what specific, recent situation was I unable to show my child unconditional love? Why not? If a similar situation were to arise again, would I attempt to respond

differently? What would help me to do so?

- In what specific, recent situation was I able to demonstrate love in spite of my child's behavior? What impact did my response have on my child?
- Do I attempt to treat all my children the same when it comes to demonstrations of love? If not, why?
- Do my actions toward my children promote or inhibit the development of healthy self-esteem?

* * * * *

Before we leave the topic of love, I would like to address my concern about a growing trend I have seen among parents of young children. I believe the term "unconditional love" is much too frequently equated with an indulgent parenting style. No child truly benefits from copious possessions and yet many parents seem hesitant to deny their children of anything for which they nag.

Let's pause a moment on this point to consider how society has glorified the accumulation of things. Sadly, many parents have fallen into the bigger-and-better trap and believe they are "demonstrating love" by buying their children stuff. Children have learned the art of masterfully controlling their parents' wallets by preying on their weaknesses, such as some parents' apparent inability to say "no." The supposition that affection is demonstrated through the giving of "stuff" is a notion that has a great, and potentially devastating, impact on young children's future beliefs and value systems. Where and why did we begin believing that a trip to the store should routinely involve buying something for our children?

About now, some of you are wondering if I am totally unaware that exchanging gifts has been identified and justifiably recognized as a "love language."[10] You argue, legitimately, that while some persons feel loved through verbal expressions or acts of service, others prefer receiving something that they can see and touch. But hear me out. The concept of love languages reinforces and complements, rather than negates, my point. A gift, given at an appropriate time and prompted by love, is a wonderful expression of affection. By contrast, buying stuff for our children simply because they nag until we are exhausted, or because we feel guilty if we don't, is not really demonstrating love at all. On the contrary, it may be encouraging character patterns of self-centeredness, self-indulgence and ingratitude. When children's appetites become insatiable they view their wishes as entitlements. This sort of thinking, instilled in the early years and repeatedly reinforced, becomes increasingly difficult to reverse over time. Remember that often the most loving thing we can say to our children is an unequivocal "no."

Respect

As noted earlier, loving children unconditionally and

treating them respectfully are quite inseparable, at least in my mind. One thing that never ceases to amaze and dismay me is the manner in which some parents treat their children at malls, fast-food restaurants, stores and playgrounds. No doubt you, as well as I, have observed parents yelling at, threatening, slapping and jerking around their children. Based on what I see in public, I shudder at the thought of what might happen in the privacy of their homes. Often, the parental tirade is induced by something as innocent as a child accidentally knocking merchandise off a shelf or wading through an irresistibly inviting mud puddle. At other times, children's behaviors are truly unacceptable. Even then, poor behavior is often precipitated by physical needs, such as hunger, fatigue, or boredom, all of which could have been circumvented by a sensitive parent. Regardless, children should be dealt with in a perceptive and caring manner.

Perhaps parents who engage in berating their offspring have forgotten that children are people too. Of course, young children are small and immature—that's an inherent and inevitable part of their current developmental stage. But in no way does that mean they are inferior human beings and their feelings and self-confidence are unaffected by how others treat them.

Further, children should never be manipulated by a parent on a power trip. A dad shouldn't demand that his son play football because it will give his father something to brag about at the office. A mother shouldn't expect her daughter to satisfy her own unfulfilled artistic fantasies.

As we continually show respect to our children, we demonstrate our conviction that they have feelings and worth. Thus, we support their efforts to become confident and self-regulating individuals.

Acceptance

Along with loving and respecting our children, accepting their uniqueness is absolutely essential to their emotional well-being. As frustrating and complex as it seems, a particular parenting style may be perfectly suited to one of our children and be just as ill-suited to another. Do we merely give intellectual assent to our children's differences, or does our parenting demonstrate that we truly understand the concept?

Children are born with innate traits—an artistic bent, a predisposition toward depression, intellectual prowess or stubbornness. Even though it is obvious that no two children are alike, we still struggle with parenting in a way that truly considers and accepts their individual differences. Often, when parents are frustrated (and even embarrassed) with a child, they will console themselves and assure others with comments such as "She's so different than her sister." Acceptance of our children is not synonymous with acceptance of their inappropriate behaviors. But is does mean adamantly rejecting the belief that one child is an inferior person simply because he or she does not fit our definition of a "model" child. We're human, so, of course, at times we will wonder, "Why can't she be like her sister?" or "How can he be so difficult?!" But this is a message that none of our children should ever even sense, let alone hear. What children do need, on the other hand, is consistent affirmation of their uniqueness and worth.

One of the most obvious differences among children is in their temperaments. Like other biological traits, such as the color of their hair and eyes, children have no control over the temperaments with which they are born. This knowledge alone should be enough to make us more accepting of our children's unique qualities and more willing to make necessary adaptations to meet their needs.

Our children come into the world with a particular set of characteristics that affects how they feel inside and how they view the world around them. Does your baby startle easily or calmly relax despite loud noises? Does your toddler quietly observe peers or aggressively and actively take charge? Does your preschooler bound out of bed in the morning ready to take on the world or sleepily drag out of bed expecting the world to meet his needs? Children's temperaments determine whether they are active or passive, attentive or distractible, noisy or quiet, cautious or eager, adaptable or resistant and happy or melancholy.

Although some children's temperaments are more challenging for parents, we must remember that every child, just as every adult, has both strengths and limitations. The key to raising healthy, well-adjusted children is to attempt to adapt their environments to best meet their individual needs. Bottom line? The contexts in which our children live either enhance their assets and diminish their liabilities, or *vice versa*.

We would be somewhat less than honest to deny that unhappy and uncooperative children greatly try the souls of even the most patient, committed and optimistic parents. But let me offer some encouragement to those of you who believe that some of the not-too-positive adjectives apply to your child. First, biology is only one factor that determines a child's development. As noted above, the environments in which our children are raised play an immense role in determining who they become. As a very simple example, providing a shy child with opportunities to socialize helps her to become self-confident and out-going. Second, qualities that are frustrating and difficult to deal with in our children may actually serve them very well. We all know of strong-willed children who accomplish great feats, highly sensitive children who exhibit amazing creativity and slow-to-adapt children who stand firm in the face of peer influence.

The concept of "intelligent empathy" is very meaningful as we consider accepting our children's temperaments and adapting accordingly. Based on truly trying to understand our children, intelligent empathy is "firmly believing that what the child does and says makes sense if approached from the child's point of view."[11] This is not an easy concept to put into practice. Consider how difficult it is to step back and objectively assess a two-year-old's reasons for repeatedly attempting to bathe the new puppy in the toilet bowl.

If we truly accept our children unconditionally, we will avoid the temptation to plan their futures by attempting to fit them into some preformed mold that satisfies our aspirations, pride and concept of ideal. Our plans, hopes and dreams must be continually tempered by a realistic appraisal of our child's capabilities, needs and preferences and the focus must be his or her ultimate good. Sadly, many adolescents and adults bear psychological scars resulting from their parents' efforts to force them to become someone they weren't meant to be. Always falling short of parental expectations, they live life feeling unfulfilled, thwarted, insignificant and maybe even worthless.

Mutual love, acceptance and respect form the foundation of a healthy family. Without these qualities, a family bears some similarities to a ship that is aimlessly adrift, while its egocentric, stubborn and arrogant crew members are consumed with self-serving agendas.

Six
DECIPHERING MORSE CODE

*The most important thing in communication
is to hear what isn't being said.*

- Peter F. Drucker[1]

Few of us would deny that communication lies at the heart of relationships. After 38 years of marriage, my husband and I still frequently find ourselves communicating poorly with each other. As we attempt to unravel misunderstandings, I'm always amazed at the discrepancy between what I said ("Make sure you pick out a nice head of lettuce") and what he heard ("Don't buy lettuce unless it's nice"). Whether it is between friends, spouses, siblings, employer and employee or parent and child, effective communication is a key to understanding, supporting and accepting others. In this chapter, we will discuss some principles that can help facilitate constructive communication between parents and their children.

One of our sons developed verbal skills at a particularly early age. He chattered incessantly as a preschooler, providing running commentaries on everything within his small world of experience and asking endless "why" questions. He was especially talkative at the dinner table, in the presence of what he perceived to be a captive audience. I recall that at times his stories were quite lengthy and disjointed, and his "jokes," evidence of his creative but still immature cognitive skills, weren't very humorous. But what I remember most is how intensely important it was to him to have everyone's undivided attention when he was speaking. If he were interrupted, his eyes would well with tears, readily revealing his sense of dismay—and maybe even betrayal. I regret that I wasn't always patient and attentive as our young son was trying out his budding communication skills. In hindsight, listening to him should have been a much higher priority than making sure the green beans were passed or the table was cleared promptly.

Listening just doesn't seem to come naturally, a reality that enhances rather than lessens its value. Effectively listening to our young children establishes a critical precedent for connecting with them as teens. In regard to the latter, it appears that parents are not doing so well. In a survey of 10,000 adolescents, nearly half said that communication with one or more parents is a very serious problem for their generation.[2] Similarly, as I've talked to adolescents whose relationships with their parents were strained if not severed, a common theme continually emerged: communication simply was not good. Let me share some examples.

Mike depicted conversation with his parents as "a dull roar"; Bob, as "yelling"; and Rebecca, as "high pitched screaming, not communicating." According to other respondents, parent-teen conversation of any sort, good or bad, was scarce and/or superficial. Regarding her family, Sara said, "We never were good at talking to each other . . . . We definitely didn't communicate a lot . . . . Communication wasn't very big in my family . . . we'd kind of keep things, like, surface." According to Ali, communication with her parents was non-existent. She put it this way: "We didn't communicate at all. They were just two people that I lived with."

Effective and constructive communication between any two persons involves both receiving and sending messages. We will begin with a discussion of receiving messages.

Receiving our Children's Messages

The first principle for receiving messages is stated very succinctly in James 1:19: "Everyone should be quick to listen."[3] As alluded to earlier, listening seems to run counter to human nature. How do we measure up as parents? One author writes,

> Determining how effective you are as a listener takes a great deal of honesty and humility. You have to be willing to quiet down and listen to yourself as you jump in and interrupt someone. Or you have to be a little more patient and observe yourself as you walk away, or begin thinking of something else, before the person you are speaking to has finished.[4]

I definitely recognize my tendency (understatement) to jump in, interrupt, or let my mind wander. How about you? Do we really think it's okay to interrupt or show obvious impatience when our children are speaking to us? If so, why? Because they aren't very articulate? Because they are smaller than we? Because we think our time is too valuable to be wasted on relatively unimportant matters? In reality, not listening undermines any attempt to unconditionally love, accept and respect our children.

Listening to our children requires us to give of something we consider very valuable—our time. Realizing that the first few seconds set the tone for any conversation, we need to discipline ourselves to send an unequivocal message when they begin speaking: yes, I am listening. This requires making eye contact and conveying with our body language that we are attentively ready to hear whatever they are about to say. Failure to do so may be sending another, very unintended, message—that we don't care about what they are saying. The following statement seems to put the whole concept of listening in perspective: "The first duty of love is to listen."[5] What a great reminder of its importance in the context of relationships.

Parents are rightfully excited when their babies begin making their first sounds. We prompt and encourage (and report to anyone who will listen) every attempt at speech. We are particularly delighted with any semblance of "mama" or "dada." But once children's speech becomes commonplace and profuse, listening becomes increasingly more difficult. By the time most children are preadolescents, they have begun saying things we don't want to hear in a manner we don't want them to be said. Although we know that the importance of listening never diminishes, it seems the ability and desire to do so decreases dramatically as our children grow up.

As adolescents talked with me, frustration with their parents regarding the matter of listening was evident. When asked whether he felt he communicated well with his parents, Steve replied, "I tried. But [they have] selective hearing. They hear what they want to hear." Liz felt that her mother's interrupting to ask questions hindered their conversations. She said she wanted to say, "Mom, just listen to the whole thing, and then ask questions if you need to."

Besides listening—carefully, that is—we need to listen beyond our children's words and attempt to determine what they are feeling. Throughout the New Testament, Jesus models this sort of listening. For example, the Bible records the story of Jesus being surrounded by a crowd of people at the home of two sisters, Mary and Martha. Many people had come to hear Him teach and Martha was busy preparing food and attending to the needs of their guests. Meanwhile, Mary was attentively sitting at Jesus' feet. Feeling overwhelmed and annoyed, Martha asked, "Lord, don't you care that my sister has left me to do the work by myself? Tell her to help me!" In Jesus' response, he identified and acknowledged her feelings: "Martha, Martha, you are worried and upset about many things."[6] By this statement, he was both validating her feelings and helping her to recognize the source of her frustration.

As parents, we need to become adept at listening for what our children are attempting to convey. For example, should a statement "I don't ever want to play baseball again" be taken at face value? Or, should it possibly be interpreted as, "I felt really embarrassed today when I let the ball go over my head," or "You need to tell me that you think I'm doing okay at third base," or "Some guys on the team are making fun of me and I don't want to be around them." Depending on what our child is actually saying, a response of "Don't be silly. Of course you want to play!" may indicate that we aren't really listening at all.

Years ago in the waiting room of a dentist's office, I heard a conversation that seemed to typify failure of a parent to listen to her son and attempt to understand his feelings. The young boy, whom I guessed to be about age four, was sitting in the chair next to his mother. She was quite engrossed in reading a magazine; by contrast, he had nothing to distract or entertain him. After sitting quietly for a few minutes, he asked his mother a simple question on an issue that was obviously of great concern: "Mommy is he going to pull my teeth out?" No response. With slightly increased intensity, he asked again, "Mommy, is he going to pull my teeth out?" Still no response. And then, a bit louder and with a tone that could not easily be ignored, he tried once again. "Mommy, is he going to pull my teeth out?" At this point, with her eyes still riveted on the magazine, his mother shook her head "no." After sitting there quietly and thoughtfully for a few minutes, the little guy obviously still had some apprehension. "Is it my turn?" he asked. Predictably, there was no response. "Is it my turn?" No response. Still politely, but with increased intensity, he asked again. "Is it my turn?" No answer. "How we gonna know when it's my turn?" Silence. "How we gonna know when it's my turn, huh?" No reply. One final time, he asked, "How we gonna know when it's my turn?" No response. The small boy finally gave up and slumped back into the chair, apparently willing to retreat within himself and contemplate what might be.

At that moment, I wanted so desperately to pull that little boy up on my lap, hug him tightly, and quiet his trepidation. He was asking great "when" and "what" questions, indicating that he had the cognitive ability to process more information than he had been given. So, why hadn't the mother made some effort to inform and reassure him? Couldn't she hear the distress in his voice? What, if anything, had she told him before they arrived at the dentist's office? How simple it would have been, I thought, for her to explain in simple terms what was, and what was not, likely to happen. How simple to answer his questions and calm his anxiety. How simple for her to suggest he pick out a child's book so that she could read to him, thus diverting his attention while he waited. How much effort could it have taken for her to give him a hug? Surely she could tell that he desperately needed to be consoled.

How easy for me to sit across the waiting room and think poorly of that mother, wanting to snatch the little boy and compensate for her apparent deficiencies. In reality, I will never know why this mother seemed to be so insensitive. Perhaps she had already told him a thousand times (at least in her mind) what was going to happen—or that she didn't *know* what was going to happen. Perhaps she had trained herself to totally tune out his incessant jabber, having determined that was a better option than yelling at him in frustration. Maybe she was normally a very sensitive mother but, as a result of what psychologists sometimes call "pile-up," she was dealing with emotional overload and her coping reservoir was depleted. Or, perhaps, she simply did not understand the importance of recognizing and acknowledging her child's feelings.

Regardless of the reasons this mother treated her son as she did on that particular day, if their interaction was typical there's reason for concern about their relationship and communication patterns during his adolescent years. As we turn once again to teens for their testimonials, we discover, not surprisingly, that those with whom I spoke didn't feel that conversations between them and their parents were substantive *or* sensitive in nature. Tonya expressed it this way: "[My parents and I] don't really talk. Unless… we're just like out to dinner or something like that. We never talk about stuff that is bothering me or whatever . . . . We didn't do that." Likewise, Steve said, "Well, for the last maybe year or so . . . they really almost never ask me how I'm doing, it's just in certain areas. Like, 'If you need to say something, we're here.' But then they never are when I need to."

We all would readily agree that listening to children is a key ingredient to effective communication. Tiny infants are eager to let their parents know when they are hungry, tired or experiencing some other source of discomfort. We as parents learn to read their verbal and non-verbal cues, anxiously attempting to determine what they are trying to "say" so we can respond in an appropriate fashion. If we feed a child who is sleepy rather than hungry, a communication breakdown has occurred. In the first months of our children's lives they are totally dependent on us to "listen" and understand. As they become toddlers and preschoolers they begin to add speech, one word or phrase at a time, to their mode of communication. Except for the very shy and introverted, three-year-olds happily chat about anything and everything.

During the first few years of life, attentive and responsive listening establishes a pattern of welcoming child-parent communication. Openness invites further communication;

conversely, being closed discourages our children from continuing (or maybe even starting) to speak. In addition to our words, our body language needs to convey, "I'm listening, I want to understand, and I care." As an example, let's suppose that when it is time to get dressed for preschool, a child says, "I don't want to go today." An open response, consistent with listening for feelings as discussed above (e.g., "Can you tell me why you don't want to go to school?"), would attempt to probe into the reasons for the child's statement. By contrast, closed responses tend to take control of the situation. These usually consist of giving commands (e.g., "It doesn't matter if you want to go; just hurry up and get dressed"); pretending there is no problem (e.g., "Of course you want to go. You love preschool"); or offering an expedient "solution" (e.g., "You'll be fine once you get there"). Consistently responding to children in a closed manner sends the message that the adult is in charge and the child's thoughts and feelings are insignificant and unimportant. As 17-year-old Opie told me, "I think [my parents] would hear what I was saying but they could never level my view with their own. It would be like, 'Well, you know what, that's nice but hey, this is what the deal is.' It always comes back to, 'This is what mom and dad say. And it's right because mom and dad say it. And that's the way it's going to be.'"

Clear communication becomes increasingly tough as children get older and discussion topics become more complex and potentially confrontational. Inviting communication from our children when they are young sets the stage for meaningful and healthy interaction during the teen years when more is at stake than whether the child wears a blue or white shirt to school. When asked if she talked with her parents when her life wasn't going well, 15-year-old Rebecca responded, "No, I'd usually ask my friends for advice whenever something bad happened. 'Cause I didn't want . . . an adult's advice!" Then she added, quietly and thoughtfully, "If I had had adult advice I'd probably have done a lot better."

* * * * *

How do we rate ourselves on the critical matter of listening to our children? On a scale of 1-10, with 10 being perfect (for any of us not prone to the pitfalls of humanity), what scores would we give ourselves?

- Do we physically focus on our children by getting on their level?
- Do we make eye contact?
- Do we display open body language that invites communication?
- Do our facial expressions convey respect?
- Do we listen patiently?
- Do we block out potential distractions to concentrate on what our children are saying?
- Do we refrain from interrupting or rushing them when

they are speaking?

- Do we attempt to look past our children's words and interpret the true meaning of what they are saying?
- Do we encourage children to express, rather than suppress, their thoughts?
- Do we listen with empathy when our children are troubled?
- Do we attempt to discover the root of children's behavior and statements rather than superficially treating the symptoms?

Once again, in this whole business of parenting, we are faced with something that's much easier said than done. If we can give ourselves 6s, and maybe 7s, it means we're doing some things reasonably well. We just need to be consciously working towards 8s, 9s, and maybe even an occasional 10.

Sending Messages to our Children

Above we quoted a portion of a Bible verse, "Everyone should be quick to listen."[7] The next phrase of that verse complements the first: "[Everyone should be] slow to speak."[8] The key to not speaking hastily is developing the practice of thinking first. (For some temperaments, this comes fairly easily. For others, it requires painstaking self-discipline. Again, I know from personal experience.) How many times have we said something thoughtlessly and wished we could take it back? Once spoken, taking words back is as difficult as putting toothpaste from the bristles of our toothbrush back into the tube. Speaking too quickly seems to be a much more common occurrence than being slow too slow to reply. Pausing, taking a deep breath, saying a quick prayer for wisdom, and considering our options helps us gain some perspective, whereas hasty retorts are emotionally generated. I would like to think that as I have gotten older I've learned to be more reflective and less reactive, but being slow to speak is still far from second nature for me. (I was recently interviewed by a reporter of the local newspaper and, knowing my comments may appear in front-page print the next day, I found myself choosing my words very carefully. Not only I, but everyone with whom I communicate, would benefit from my routinely practicing such deliberate, thoughtful speech.)

I suspect that very few of us could say with integrity that we always control our speech. Sadly, the ones we love the most—our family—generally bear the brunt of our thoughtless and disrespectful words. In a Biblical passage that never ceases to bring me personal conviction, James writes, "With the tongue we praise our Lord . . . and curse men, who have been made in God's likeness. Out of the same mouth come praise and cursing. My brothers [and sisters], this should not be."[9] And then, as if that weren't condemning enough, the writer adds a piercing question: "Can both fresh water and salt water flow from the same spring?"[10] On the same note, I often think of the words of Amy Carmichael, "If a sudden jar can cause me to speak an impatient, unloving word, then I know nothing of Calvary love. (For a cup brimful of sweet water cannot spill even one drop of bitter water however suddenly jolted.)"[11]

Surely these cautions don't apply to the way we speak to our children! After all, at some point even "model" children are annoying and disobedient; of course, *they'll* bring out the worst in us. The reality is that it is not okay to adopt a misguided double standard when it comes to our relationship with adults versus those with our children. We should no more scold a child for accidentally spilling milk on the kitchen floor than we would a friend for spilling tea on the living room sofa.

Children should be expected to behave in a childish manner. We, on the other hand, should be held to a higher standard—both because we are adults and because our children are watching us. As Paul says, "When I was a child, I talked like a child, I thought like a child, I reasoned like a child. When I became a man, I put childish ways behind me."[12] One gauge of our maturity (or lack thereof) is the manner in which we talk to our children.

Another important principle when dealing with children's behavior is this: whenever possible, messages should be given in the first person ("I . . .) rather than the second ("You . . .).[13] Admittedly, when we are frustrated or upset by another, the natural reaction is an accusation that begins with "you." But take a moment to contrast "What are *you* thinking—tromping in the house and getting mud all over the floor I just scrubbed!" and "*I* feel frustrated when the floor *I* just scrubbed gets all muddy." "You" messages tend to blame others while "I" messages express the speaker's thoughts and feelings. Generally, the former make our children defensive and resistant while the latter help them to develop empathy and become more aware of others' feelings. Although sending "I," rather than "you," messages isn't instinctive for most of us, it *can* be acquired through practice.

One final thought regarding sending messages to our children. Children, even at very young ages, can acquire a malady called "parent deafness"--just, as noted above, parents can become child deaf. How often have we heard a parent commanding a child to do something and we knew absolutely the child was not going to comply? The parent knew too, but, out of habit, was prepared to repeat the message in an increasingly demanding manner, gradually adding threats, until the child at least acknowledged he was being addressed. Many children don't obey initially because they've learned to predict the precise point at which parents actually mean what they are saying (e.g., when "Tommy" becomes "Thomas" and then "Thomas Edward"). Children are much more likely to obey if we follow the old adage to "say what we mean and mean what we say"—the first time.

Another key to minimizing children's parent deafness is to get the child's attention before we speak. Children, who are by nature fascinated, curious, and easily distracted by their environment, seldom tune in immediately to a parent's voice. We can save both our children and ourselves a great deal of frustration by making sure that we, rather than the tiny brown ants that are busily building a dwelling in the sidewalk cracks, have their attention. A good way to begin communication with a child is by making eye contact and asking, "Are you listening?"

A final suggestion regarding helping our children hear, understand, and respond is to follow our statements by a simple question: "What did I say?" This practice lessens the probability of miscommunication and enhances accountability. If children repeat, "I need to pick up my toys and put them on the shelf before I can go outside to play," they are less likely to contend that they didn't hear or understand what they were expected to do.

* * * * *

Here are some questions that will serve as a self-check on sending messages to our children:

- Am I likely to speak hastily and wish I hadn't? Or do I remain quiet until I am composed and can respond in a thoughtful manner?
- Based on the way I speak to my children, would I be considered a mature or immature individual?

- When I am upset with my children, am I more likely to calmly send "I" messages ("I feel . . .") or angrily send "You" messages ("You always . . .")?
- Do my children have parent deafness? If so, why? What specific steps can I take to attempt to minimize it?
- Do I ask my children to repeat my words to make certain they have understood what I have said?

* * * * *

Perhaps the most important principle of communication really doesn't have to do with sending and receiving messages. Rather, it has to do with the state of our hearts. As we are reminded in the New Testament, "Out of the overflow of the heart the mouth speaks."[14] And, just as we speak from our hearts, we listen with our hearts. Trying to change the way we listen and speak, without first changing our heart attitude, is quite futile.

Finally, assuming you are as human as I, don't be too disillusioned if you don't always communicate with your children the way you'd like to or know you should. Two little words, "I'm sorry," let our children know that sometimes we mess up too. By asking their forgiveness, we are modeling two additional character traits we'd like our children to possess: humility and a willingness to admit our mistakes.

Seven
THE CHAIN OF COMMAND

Too many parents make life hard for their children by trying,
too zealously, to make it easy for them.

- Johann von Goethe[1]

On a ship, the buck stops with its captain. In order for a vessel to successfully navigate and safely reach its intended destination, each crew member, whether first mate or ordinary seaman, must abide not only by the rules of the sea but the rules of his or her captain. The corresponding analogy to the family is obvious. Just as the Captain must assume responsibility for the overall operations of a ship, so parents must maintain command of their family's ship. And, with all due respect to every great captain of the sea, I suspect that keeping a family on course may make guiding a ship seem effortless by comparison.

Of all topics that parents are anxious to discuss, discipline is consistently among the most common. Parents, weary of frustrating and exhausting daily hassles, want to be told specifically what to do when their two-year-old rubs applesauce into his hair, ears, and eyes, carefully avoiding his mouth. The fact that this is considered normal toddler behavior is only minimally comforting to a parent who is feeling totally out-maneuvered by a 19-pounder in pull-ups. So, how should we advise these parents? Relax, see the humorous side, and remember he'll grow out of this messy stage before you know it? Give him another helping of applesauce, assist him in holding his spoon, and praise any attempt to actually get the food in the vicinity of his mouth? Firmly but calmly explain to him that his behavior is unacceptable and a repeat performance will result in his not getting applesauce again until he learns to eat properly? Run to get the camera to preserve this moment for posterity? Immediately whisk him to the bathtub, scrub him down, and put him to bed? Ignore him and retreat to your own "happy place"? So many options, but how do we determine what is best for that particular parent and child on that particular day?

Many times each day, without the luxury of a trusted personal parenting consultant standing by, parents make decisions about if, how, and when to discipline their children. Interestingly, much discipline is based on a parent's current mood, circumstances and level of stress as opposed to the child's behavior. If you are feeling relaxed, with time to recognize and appreciate your toddler's playful ingenuity, you might perceive the applesauce incident as an amusing photo op. On the other hand, if you simply must leave the house in ten minutes and you have yet to get a morning shower, patience and humor are difficult, if not impossible, to conjure up. Given the degree of variability within any household at any given moment, how does a parent maintain proper balance and "captain" status?

Who's in charge?

Through the years, others have referred to me as a child advocate and defender of youth. Based on what you have read up to this point, I suspect you might agree with these categorizations. I am greatly disturbed when children are dishonored and disrespected simply because they've had less time to mature and be socialized in a manner acceptable to the adults in their lives. Now let me deal with a related issue, which could be considered the flip side of the coin.

Treating children fairly and respectfully is one thing; allowing them to *control* the authority figures in their lives is quite another. Somehow, it seems to me that many of today's parents have confused the two. They seem to believe, or at least act as if they believe, that it is appropriate for children to be in charge. (Could a ship find its way with an ordinary seaman at the helm?) I have often suggested to parents that they place a reminder on their refrigerator that states, "I am the parent, s/he is the child," lest they forget. I sadly acknowledge that there seems to be some legitimacy in the words of Edward VIII, Duke of Windsor, a half century ago. He observed, "The thing that impresses me most about Americans is the way parents obey their children."[2]

Most homes can be characterized, to varying degrees, as

either child-controlled or parent-controlled. In homes in which children are in charge, parents are frazzled and exhausted by their children's continual wants and demands. In-charge children, whose manipulative behaviors may include whining, nagging, belligerence and tantrums, have learned how to get their parents to obey. But children are not really to blame for this unfortunate role reversal; they have only taken control because their parents have relinquished it. That's why there is so much frustration and tension in homes where children are fed whenever they say they're hungry but aren't required to eat reasonable amounts at family meal-time; where they are allowed to skip nap-time, no matter how tired and cranky, because they protest so vehemently; and where they are discontented unless they are being entertained by someone or some form of media.

Although limited and appropriate child-choice teaches children to make responsible decisions, young children should not be given numerous options about anything. In amazement, I have observed parents allowing three-year-olds to pick out any pair of shoes they want to buy, with literally dozens from which to choose. What kind of concept does a 3-year-old have of function, practicality, comfort, or economy? Children simply aren't good at being in charge. Why? There's no way they can possibly know what's best for them. As one psychologist writes, "Wisdom comes only from experience—the big thing a child is short on."[3]

Distinguishing between child- and parent-controlled families isn't particularly tough for an outside observer. However, accurately evaluating one's own family can be quite difficult—particularly because no adult cares to admit to being manipulated by a child.

* * * * *

To attempt to honestly assess who's in charge at your house, take a moment to answer the following questions:

- Do your children procrastinate, argue, and question instructions and rules? Do they commonly continue to nag after you have said "no"? Do you routinely engage in debate and compromise, or give in to their demands?
- Do you tell your children certain consequences will occur but then not follow through?
- Do you frequently put your children's demands for attention above your own responsibilities and needs?
- When you go somewhere without your children, do you feel you should bring them a gift to compensate for leaving them?
- Do you offer your child too many choices and allow him or her to make decisions that you should be making?

* * * * *

Around eighteen to twenty-four months is when most toddlers begin to seriously "test the waters" in a quest to determine who's in charge. If you are expecting your first child, or your child is still an infant, now is the time to step up to the plate, so to speak, and determine to have a home in which children obey their parents, rather than *vice versa*. Needless to say, this is much easier said than done. There are several parental factors that make being in charge particularly difficult for some parents, such as a meek, highly sensitive, or relaxed personality; a tendency to avoid conflict at all cost; an exaggerated desire to be "needed" as a parent; and current or past troubled relationships with one's own parents. Additionally, there are child characteristics, such as being strong-willed, and familial factors, such as divorce, that increase the likelihood children will control their parents. If any, some, or most of these characteristics describe your situation, you may be particularly vulnerable to being controlled by your children. I kindly encourage you to avoid being caught in this trap, which is detrimental to you, your child, and the relationship between you.

If you sense that you have already lost control to and of your children, take heart. It is not too late to change. You can make a commitment right now to reclaim your rightful and essential place as authority in your child's life. It can be done, and there are several compelling reasons to do so. First, the Bible clearly instructs children to obey their parents: "Children, obey your parents . . . for this is right."[4] For families to function properly, that's the way it must be. When children disobey their parents, they are also disobeying a much higher power—God Himself. Second, bear in mind that children who have too much decision-making power are less likely to mature well, especially in the areas of social and emotional development. Third, parents who have a sense of control are less stressed and frustrated, and thus are better able to meet the genuine needs of their families. Finally, as I have noted throughout this book, the patterns of control formed during early childhood will very likely carry over into the teen years, when the stakes are much higher than whether a child washes his hands before dinner.

Now let's turn again to the teens with whom I visited and get their perspective on the matter of parental authority. Perhaps you are surprised to learn that a consistently recurring theme was that their parents should have been stricter. Sara recalled that her parents "started off" giving her a lot of freedom and that's where she had a chance to "mess up." Bailey said that if her parents had enforced the rules she would not have ended up at a residential facility for troubled teens. Mike told of growing marijuana in his room, and when I asked if his parents knew what was going on, he replied,

> "Oh yeah, I mean . . . [my parents] took it away, but they didn't do anything about it. I would have expected them to like call the police or something but . . . they didn't do anything about it . . . I wish they had said, "You're not going to do this, you're not going to do that."

Then there was George, who told me about the time he got drunk, overdosed, passed out, and threw up on a cop's feet. He woke up in his own bed, and speculated, "I guess my mom put me there." He added incredulously that his parents never talked to him about the incident.

We can safely assume that at the same time these teens were making poor choices regarding risky and antisocial behaviors, they were sending a plethora of decisive messages to their parents to discourage them from involvement. Their verbal as well as nonverbal communication likely indicated, "I want to be my own person," "I don't need you to tell me what to do" and "I don't care what you think." And yet, in retrospect, they clearly wished their parents *had* taken control. This is still another reminder that parents need to be committed to optimum rules of parenting, based on sound principles, rather than the messages their children are sending.

The Ultimate Objective

Much like deciding our destination before we embark upon a journey, we need to understand our purpose for discipline before determining appropriate guiding principles. Why do we discipline our children? First, let's attempt to understand what "discipline" is—and what it is not. Discipline comes from the root word "disciple," which means to follow the opinions or teachings of another.[5] Discipline is all about training our children by passing along a belief system of standards and morals whereby they can live. And, if nothing else stays with you after you've read this discussion of discipline, I hope you'll remember this one principle, which I believe to be foundational to all others: *the ultimate objective of discipline is self-regulation.* We should discipline in order to "teach [our] children all they will need to know to function well as adults; things such as the important correlation between their behavior and its consequences (both good and bad), the concepts of accountability and responsibility, and appropriate ways to solve problems and make good choices."[6] Do we get it? Discipline is training children so that they no longer need external influences, such as parental instructions or demands, to do what is right; rather, an internal belief system kicks in to guide their thoughts and actions.

To take this one step further, a true disciple doesn't just blindly follow the mentor's doctrine, but truly believes in it. This brings us to another critical component of discipline: discretion. We as parents are not to pass along a hodge-podge of ideas that may or may not have merit. Rather, we are to pass along the beliefs to which we adhere, in which we firmly believe. The notion here is that we as parents have already sifted and sorted and come to conclusions about how life should be lived. When parents tell me they are not going to teach their children how to believe, but rather they want their children to "explore all options" (in matters such as moral values, lifestyle, and religion), it appears that there is an absence of parental "discipline," in the true sense of the word.

In stark contrast to discipline, punishment is "pain, suffering, or loss that serves as retribution"; "severe, rough, or disastrous treatment."[7] Discipline is proactive; punishment is reactive and there is a quite apparent negative correlation between the two. The more effectively a child is disciplined, the less necessary is punishment (and *vice versa*).

As Englishman Charles Kingsley said, "There are two freedoms: the false where one is free to do what he likes, and the true where he is free to do what he ought."[8] The goal of discipline is self-regulation, which means that our children will grow up to do what they ought.

We all know that it is common for young children to balk when asked to comply with straightforward, everyday requests: pick up your toys, put on your shoes, come to the dinner table, get in the car. What, if any, guidelines can effectively and consistently direct spur-of-the-moment, as well as more pragmatic, decisions about discipline? The suggestions that follow pertain only partially to our children. For the most part, they have to do more with our attitudes and behaviors than those of our offspring.

One of the keys to effective discipline is that, rather than going along with the popular or trendy advice of the day, we make decisions based on the big picture—the person our children will someday become. (Remember setting goals? Charting the course? This is exactly why it matters.) This approach requires that our children understand that there are both privileges and responsibilities inherent in being a part of the Smith, Jones or Jackson family. Regardless of whether this condition is viewed positively or negatively, it is a fact of life. For our family, expectations placed on our children included living by the rules of the Mumford household. I still vividly remember the sight of our small son sitting dejectedly on the curb, slumped shoulders, elbows on knees, and chin in the palms of his hands. His two same-age buddies were happily riding their "big wheel" tricycles in the street. He, on the other hand, was only allowed to ride in our driveway. He could view this situation as nothing other than a travesty of justice. Our son was learning a painful truth at a very early age: like it or not, at times there would be discrepancies between his rules and those of his friends. At the time of this incident, I had no concept of how relevant this principle would become during the "everybody's doing it" teenage years.

The decision regarding the big wheel episode was quite simple and straightforward for me: in my mind, a three-year-old riding in the street posed a serious threat to his physical well-being. End of story. Although I didn't like seeing him so unhappy, I wasn't at all inclined to change my mind. It was also relatively easy to enforce his staying out of the street because our son, who was tiny enough to find a curb-height seat quite comfortable, knew the momentary rush of disobedience wasn't worth the inevitable unpleasant consequences. Additionally, he had not honed the skills of arguing persuasively, attempting to induce guilt by questioning my sense of justice, or causing me to question my own judgment. You know where I'm going with this, don't you. Variations of the tricycle episode were repeated countless times as our son (and his younger brother) experienced childhood and adolescence. Unfortunately but predictably, as situations became more complex and convoluted I sometimes lacked my previous clear-cut conviction and confidence. But, I would mentally revisit my first encounter with a parental decision at odds with those of other parents and attempt to employ the same criterion I did years earlier: what I believed to be best for our son. With that bottom line, it was much easier for me to fulfill my duties as a focused captain, rather than continually second-guessing my decisions.

Parental Warmth and Control

We've talked about treating children kindly and respectfully and about parental versus child control. Let's now focus on the role and relationship of these two aspects of parenting. Perhaps you are familiar with a time-tested and well established categorization of parenting styles, which includes the following types: uninvolved, permissive, authoritarian and authoritative.[9] Each of these four categories can be defined by two dimensions: warmth and control.[10] Warm parents are responsive, loving, accepting, and respecting. Although the word control is often interpreted as heavy-handed and dictatorial, in this context controlling parents are those with clear-cut expectations and requirements of their children.

Let's now briefly look more in-depth at the characteristics of uninvolved, permissive, authoritarian, and authoritative parents. To help us project into possible future ramifications of various parenting styles, I have included a brief summary of research findings on adolescence related to each.

Uninvolved (or indifferent) parents, whose style has little warmth *or* control, tend to be uncaring, unresponsive and unavailable to their children. They routinely neglect their children's emotional and physical needs, and, in extreme cases, they are guilty of totally rejecting their children. Parents who consistently put their own desires and needs above their children's, seldom connecting with them on a physical or emotional level, fall into this category. Research suggests that children of uninvolved parents tend to be impulsive. When these children become adolescents, they commonly engage in delinquent behaviors and experiment with drugs, sex, and alcohol.[11] [12] [13] Feeling alone and unloved, with little external monitoring or internal discipline, they tend to be impulsive and vulnerable to making poor choices.

A *permissive* or *indulgent* parenting style is characterized by warmth combined with minimal structure and monitoring. Permissively functioning homes fit into the category of "child-controlled," as discussed previously. Children have a great deal of decision-making power. They are encouraged to determine their own standards and regulate their own behaviors; seeing their parents as role models or authority figures is unimportant on their journey to "find themselves." As would be suspected, a link has been found between children of permissive parents and involvement in problem behaviors such as drug and alcohol use[14][15] and school misconduct.[16] With little training, discipline, or monitoring, these children tend to choose a carefree lifestyle, living for the pleasures of the moment with little consideration of the consequences.

Authoritarian parenting, with its "because-I-said-so" mentality, is dictatorial in style. The opposite of permissive parents, who are low on control and high on warmth, authoritarian parents are low on warmth and high on control. These parents do not offer explanations or understanding; children are expected to simply comply with parents' demands with unquestioning obedience. Authoritarian parenting is commonly associated with various adolescent risk-taking behaviors, including substance use and delinquency.[17] [18] [19] [20] [21] Because of a lack of decision-making opportunities, these children tend to be dependent and socially insecure. Engaging in potentially detrimental behaviors is often an attempt to escape excessive parental strictness and over-protectiveness.

The final parenting style, *authoritative*, is characterized by a blend of warmth and control. Authoritative parents set standards and boundaries in the context of love. They exercise firm control but remain sensitive to children's individual needs and desires. Perhaps one of the most important traits of authoritative parents is that they look beyond immediate results (such as cessation of whining and much-needed peace and quiet) to their children's long-term well-being. Compared to their peers, adolescents of authoritative parents engage in fewer problem behaviors[22] [23] [24] [25] [26] [27] and high levels of moral reasoning.[28] These children tend to be self-confident, socially adept, responsible, creative and high achieving, factors that decrease the likelihood they will engage in behaviors that are detrimental to themselves and others.[29]

As an in-class activity in a couple of the undergraduate college courses I teach, I present a parenting dilemma to the students. They must divide into small groups, discuss the problem, and role play four different responses, consistent with each of the parenting types discussed above. Time after time, the students conclude without prompting that the optimum approach, authoritative, is a lot of hard work. Much more thought and energy is required for cooperative, pragmatic discipline than for dictatorial or permissive parenting. In order to stay the course despite the time and energy required, we must continually keep our eyes focused on the purpose and prize: our children's present and future well-being.

A critical but often overlooked aspect of discipline is what occurs after disciplinary action has been taken. Assuming the crisis is past, both you and your child are relatively calm, and the child is old enough to verbalize her thoughts, this is an opportune time to ask her (a) why discipline occurred, (b) what will happen if her behavior is repeated, and (c) what she can do differently, given a similar set of circumstances, in the future. Finally, regardless of the child's age or specificity of the context, the parent has a made-to-order opportunity to exhibit unconditional love. Children of all ages need to know that, despite their actions, parental love is something of which they can always be certain.

* * * * *

As a self-check in the area of discipline, consider how you would handle these scenarios:

- Your 2-year-old has just lost the privilege of playing with a favorite toy for the fourth time today. You are feeling exasperated, disappointed, and ineffective, and exchanging your stay-at-home-parent status to become a checker at the local grocery store is starting to appeal.
- Your 3-year-old son turns bed-time into a battle of the wills. Even though he stays in bed (once he's finally

there), he yells from his room asking for a drink of water, saying he needs to go to the bathroom, and complaining that his room is too dark.

- Your 4-year-old frequently refuses to eat the meals served to the rest of the family then wants to continually snack between meals.

- Your 6-year-old son hit another child in the face with a soccer ball. You think it was an accident, but you're not sure.

- You attempt to help your 7-year-old daughter with her homework each day after school. She routinely uses every excuse possible to get out of doing it, such as saying the work is too hard, complaining of a headache, saying she's tired, and saying the teacher doesn't care whether or not she does it.

- When you take your 8-year-old son shopping, he incessantly begs you to buy the latest toys or clothes for him.

* * * * *

Maybe you aren't sure how you'd respond to some of the above-described situations, or possibly your parenting style doesn't fit neatly into one of the four parenting approaches outlined above. That's certainly no cause for concern. What matters, and what I'd like for you to remember from this discussion, is the importance of including two critical, complementary components as you discipline: *warmth* (being caring and responsive), and *control* (maintaining your role as an authority figure).

Composure

Previously we discussed parents who swat and scold their children in restaurants and on playgrounds. By exhibiting this type of behavior, they have failed to adhere to a very basic premise of effective discipline: parents being in control of their own words and actions. Parents who do not restrain and control *themselves* are certainly not in a proper state of mind to positively influence their *children's* emotions and behaviors. When adults lose their composure, parent-child interaction is reduced to nothing more than that of quarreling children. Parents who struggle with self-control need to learn how to quickly and effectively manage their own actions before addressing those of their children. One helpful guideline is to remember that anything that buys additional time and allows you to think before you react (such as slowly counting to 20, saying a prayer, putting on your favorite CD, taking 10 deep breaths, or putting yourself in "time-out") will increase the likelihood that you will discipline in a sensible manner.

When attempting to handle matters of discipline with composure, your goal is to respond in a calculated fashion, rather than to react emotionally and thoughtlessly. Firm decisiveness sets you apart as the one who is in control of not only the situation, but of yourself. As children get older, they become more and more adept at spotting, and attempting to take advantage of, parental insecurities and vulnerabilities.

Wisdom

Perhaps you've heard the expression "Experience is learning from your own mistakes; wisdom is learning from someone else's." I like this principle, but I have to admit that I struggle with its application to the task of parenting. Because every child, every family, and every set of circumstances is so unique and complex, it seems that there are many things parents simply can't learn from someone else. Rather, as much as I hate to admit it, we are forced to rely on a certain degree of trial and error in matters of discipline and training. So it is this experimentation, of sorts, that leads to conclusions about what sometimes works with some children under some conditions—and what does not. Learning from our own successes and failures, is, perhaps, the beginning of becoming wise parents.

On the topic of trial and error parenting, a dear friend with whom I shared many parenting joys and struggles joked that our first children should be throw-aways rather than real babies. She contends that we could practice, make all our mistakes, and move on to the "real" child, competent, relaxed and ready for whatever challenges lie ahead. Of course, we all know that even if were feasible to have a trial run with child #1, what we learned would likely not apply to subsequent children, given inevitable individual differences among off-spring.

No doubt, parenting can be an intimidating task. Few parents would deny their sense of inadequacy when it comes to the matter of discipline. With our little one lying in the bassinette, we would do well to echo Solomon's prayer when he was chosen as leader of the Israelites: "Give me wisdom and knowledge, that I may lead this people."[30] We all need discernment to guide our children on the journey of life. And I know of nothing that drains our reservoir of ingenuity, tolerance, and judgment quicker than the matter of disciplining our children. It is my contention that one reason it's so difficult is because they are *our* children—and we care so much.

"Save it for the Biggies"

There are a few rather simple phrases that helped guide my husband and me through years of decisions regarding discipline. One of those is "Save it for the biggies," or, phrased a bit differently, "This is not a hill to die on." Good advice, right? But even though I've attempted to adhere to this principle rather consistently, it hasn't always been easy to define a "biggie." For one thing, what seems important at one age may seem totally inconsequential at another. Should my children be expected to make their beds each morning? The answer is probably "yes" if teaching my three-year-old daughter to be disciplined and responsible is high on my priority list. However, the answer may be "no," and an unmade bed seem quite trivial, when I realize that my twelve-year-old she has been lying to me about her math grade. So, does this mean that it is okay to expect my three-year-old to make her bed, but when she is twelve it no longer matters? Does that make any sense at all?

Another issue that complicates defining a "biggie" is this: what is important to one parent or child may be totally irrelevant to or even impossible for another. As a personal example, I continually battle the tendency to be a perfectionist (which, I suspect, my family would describe as more than a tendency). When our sons were young, this translated into my expecting their rooms to be neat at all times. For one son this worked well. He, in fact, had built-in standards that made it difficult for him to go to sleep at night until everything was neatly in its place. For the other son, his having an orderly room remained an elusive expectation; years of encouragement, training, and prodding generally turned out to be discouraging if not futile. (I tried every reasonable method of discipline/training to which I had ever been exposed.) With his laid-back and light-hearted spirit, he would readily respond to being asked to clean his room. Just as cheerfully, after the expenditure of substantial time and energy, he would call to me, "Time for an inspection." When I went to his room, I was consistently amazed that he actually thought that his room was "ready for inspection" when, in fact, it appeared to me that he had used his time in the pursuit of clothes-pile rearrangement. He just didn't seem to be able to see things as I did—or as I thought he should. So, does this mean it's okay to have a certain set of standards for one child and a different set of standards for another? What about consistency and fairness? Valid questions, for sure.

Here's how I put into practice the philosophy of "saving it for the biggies." I realized that if I attempted to address everything in our children's lives that didn't meet my standards, or of which I disapproved, by the time they were thirteen they would be totally parent-deaf and I would be totally exhausted. I tried to distinguish between issues that were relatively insignificant and those that pertained to our child's character. My goal was to focus on the latter rather than the former. Again, that little rule of thumb might sound good at face value. But you are no doubt astute enough to recognize that it's not exactly a panacea. If I tell my child that I expect him to keep his room orderly, and he leaves his clothes in piles on the floor, is that an inconsequential matter (one of housekeeping standards) or an issue of character (disobedience)? I truly wish the answers to these questions were more obvious.

Childish Irresponsibility vs. Willful Defiance

Another guideline I have found extremely helpful in

determining appropriate reactions to children's behaviors is to distinguish between childish irresponsibility and willful defiance, as suggested by a child psychologist.[31] A child's *intention*, as best it can be deciphered, should dictate parental responses. As noted previously, children's and adults' behaviors shouldn't be expected to reflect the same level of maturity. Adults have a big advantage over children: they have had an opportunity to grow up. Forgetting to set the table and clumsily knocking food off the high chair tray are likely due to a child's cognitive or physical immaturity. Thus, these behaviors could rightfully be categorized as "childish irresponsibility." By contrast, consider a child's refusing to set the table because it interrupts play time or deliberately sliding food off the high chair tray as a means of demonstrating refusal to eat. These behaviors are obvious efforts to gain control by doing the opposite of what s/he has been asked or is expected to do. Thus, they can be interpreted as "willful defiance."

Determining a child's intention is an invaluable first step toward dealing with undesirable behavior. Childish irresponsibility requires understanding and patience. So does willful defiance. But, in addition, the child must receive a clear and firm message: the behavior is not acceptable and must not continue.

Boundary-setting

Much as buoys measure the appropriateness of water depth for sea-going vessels, boundaries give children parameters within which to operate. They help children distinguish between what is acceptable and unacceptable, appropriate and inappropriate, safe and unsafe, kind and unkind. A child needs to know that it is okay to accept a cookie from grandma but not from a stranger on the playground. It is acceptable to express frustration by saying "I want that toy" but not by pulling a playmate's hair to get it. Boundaries are intended to keep toddlers from pulling lamps on their heads and teenagers from getting drunk. But how does a parent even begin to set appropriate and realistic boundaries? What a seemingly overwhelming task to protect our children from the big world out there and, at times, from themselves.

At the risk of being over-simplistic, I'd like to condense the discussion of boundaries to three steps: establish, communicate, and implement. Don't we all appreciate knowing what we can and cannot do? Doesn't a capable captain plainly spell out his or her expectations to the crew? Doesn't the crew understand the consequences of falling short of those expectations?

The first step, establishing boundaries, requires that parents consider what is appropriate, realistic, and fair for each child. Should a 5-year-old be expected to come in for dinner at 6:00 without a reminder? Can we expect him to take responsibility without adult intervention? If so, we need to make certain he has a means to do so, such as an alarm on his wristwatch. So, if a wristwatch alarm works perfectly to get one 5-year-old to dinner without a hassle, will it work for all 5-year-olds? The obvious answer is "no."

Early childhood educators wisely make a distinction between *age* and *individual* appropriateness. Although guidelines based on age are helpful, individual differences make it unrealistic to have the same expectations for all children of a particular chronological age. In order to be consistently effective, even a procedure as seemingly simple as coming to dinner needs to be tailored to a child's individual temperament and abilities.

Once boundaries are established, they must be clearly communicated. The principles of sending and receiving messages, discussed above, can aid parents in making certain they and their children have the same expectations. Should the alarm be set for 5:55, allowing the child 5 minutes to come inside? Is he to be inside the back door or at the table with his hands washed by 6:00? Is it 6:00 according to his Superman wristwatch or according to the kitchen clock? Or, in keeping with the "save it for the biggies" philosophy, does getting to dinner a few minutes late really matter at all?

You are in the best position to decide what is most appropriate and effective for your child. As you contemplate this, remember that boundaries aren't primarily about dinner time.   Rather, they are about training a child—to listen, to follow instructions, and to assume responsibility for his/her own actions. Although extreme rigidity is not advisable, on the other side of the coin, ambiguity and vacillation undermine the impact and purpose of boundary-setting. And some children are particularly adept at finding and using loopholes to their advantage.

The final facet of boundaries is follow-up. When a child comes in from outside on his own and is at the dinner table at 6:00, positive reinforcement is a useful tool for encouraging the child to repeat the desired behavior the next evening. This can be as simple as "Good job getting to dinner on time," or "The meal is more enjoyable for all of us when you come to dinner with no hassle."

On the other hand, when the child steps outside the parameters of the boundaries that were established and communicated, it is time for consequences. Notice the use of the word "consequences" as opposed to punishment. Consequences are administered in a respectful manner; they are for bad choices, not bad children. A tactic that I think is very important is this: whenever possible, parents should determine and convey consequences at the same time the boundaries are being established and communicated. The ramifications of this approach, and its potential for simplifying the implementation of consequences, are huge. If a child decides to be late for dinner, he has chosen to be subjected to the pre-determined consequences, which come as no surprise. In a rather simple application of the cause and effect principle, the child, not the parent, has made the choice.

Parents tend to repeatedly fall back on the same discipline techniques—time out, sending a child to his room, grounding. Although those definitely are suitable and sometimes produce the intended results, there are many occasions when more creative and unique discipline is likely to be more effective. Commonly advocated in parenting programs,[32] a "logical consequence" is fitted to the child's behavior. Therefore, the child is more likely to connect the cause (his behavior) and the effect (the consequence he experiences). If a child does not come in for dinner on time, a logical consequence is that the family eats without him. Note that in order to plan an effective consequence, you must know your child and what matters to your child. If he doesn't care if the family eats without him, that consequence would certainly not serve its intended purpose.

Another reminder is to make sure that you can live with the discipline upon which you've decided. Setting consequences in advance, rather than at the time the offense occurs, lessens the likelihood you will impose discipline that you later regret. Regardless of whether it is predetermined or decided at the moment, once a child has been told the consequence of a certain behavior it is generally undesirable to change it. But there are exceptions to that as well.

I remember the parent of a preschooler calling me one day in a rather frantic state. The previous day she had told her son that he could not have anything else to eat until he finished his dinner. The tiny little guy seemed all too eager to engage in a battle of the wills; and, unfortunately for the parent, winning seemed to be a higher priority to him than food! When the mother called me, many hours after his initial refusal, she could not stand the thought of his going another minute without food, but she was also concerned about the future ramifications of her "giving in" to him. How had she gotten into this predicament? The consequence was logical, wasn't it? All he had to do is finish his dinner! She never imagined such a clash would ensue. The lesson here is that children, especially the determined variety, should never be underestimated.

How do parents avoid this sort of quandary? I suggest never using essentials, such as food, as bargaining chips. However, if you do find yourself facing a lose-lose situation such as the one just described, try to put it in the perspective of the big picture. This is one relatively minor, albeit seemingly unsalvageable, incident and it does not mean you've failed as a parent. I believe when it becomes clear that your child, rather than you, has assumed a dominant position in a battle of the wills, it is best to simply say, "I have changed my mind. Instead of your not getting anything else to eat until you have eaten what's on your plate, I have decided that you will not be allowed to . . ." Although the child shrewdly took control and avoided one particular consequence, he is faced with another one which, hopefully, you will be able to enforce.

Both in establishing and enforcing boundaries, as children get older "fairness" becomes an increasingly bigger issue. A simple rule is to be certain that we are not asking something of our children with which they *can* not, rather than *will* not, comply. Realistic expectations are a must if we want to avoid resentment regarding the parent-child power differential and/or an absolute refusal to obey.

Besides being realistic, another way to minimize protests of "it's not fair" is to have our children involved in establishing boundaries and determining the consequences of overstepping them. Family meetings, which will be discussed in more detail in a few pages, can serve as a forum for developing and documenting family rules.

Needless to say, no matter how thoughtful and painstaking our approach to discipline, there will be times when we are caught off guard and are struggling with whether the boundaries and their consequences are equitable. Asking our children what they think is a legitimate approach. But, lest we regard getting their input as a panacea, let me share with you just a couple of instances when our sons and I disagreed about boundaries and I elicited help from them.

I remember when one of our sons was telling me that I was being unfair to not let him go somewhere with his friends. At this point I apparently was feeling I wasn't on very solid ground, and I wasn't sure how to respond. Wanting him to consider it from my perspective and give me his input, I said, "Let's reverse roles. I'm the child. I think you're being unfair not to let me go." Much to my surprise and dismay, he responded, "But I said it's *fine* if you go."

Just to let you know that not just one but both of our sons were capable of out-maneuvering me, I also recall trying to get the other son's input in a decision related to discipline. I asked him, "What would you do if you were the parent and I was the child?" Without a second's hesitation, he answered, "I'd ask you what would do would do if you were the parent and I was the child." So much for getting help from them!

Monitoring

Where does monitoring enter the picture? When children are little, monitoring means making sure they don't put their fingers into electrical outlets or chase a ball into the street. When they're elementary age, we make certain they are ready for their spelling quiz and they actually turn off their bedroom lights somewhere near the agreed-upon time. Beyond the specifics, though, monitoring is conveying the sense to our children that there's someone to whom they answer and there is someone who cares whether or not they comply with the family's standards. Children who are not mature enough to consistently monitor their own behaviors need assistance to do so. As adults, we refer to this concept as accountability.

Once again, as children get older the stakes become higher. Rather than a matter of their being tired at school because they turned the light off at 8:27 rather than 8:00, ignoring an 11:00 curfew could lead to late-night opportunities to get into serious trouble. Parental monitoring is protective. In fact, research indicates that parental monitoring makes teens less likely to make poor choices such as abusing substances[33] and engaging in premarital sexual activity.[34]

Now for some final remarks regarding discipline. A pattern that I've seen played out many times is the tendency for parents to be caught off guard when their children become 11, 12, or 13 and start making choices and displaying behaviors contrary to what they have been taught. In defense of parents, it really is quite disconcerting when a perfectly behaved and loving child begins acting so different. For instance, when a 12-year-old would rather hang out at the mall on Friday evening than participate in the family's movie and popcorn ritual, dismay and concern are not unpredictable parental responses. Remember that this is the time for logic and reason (e.g., "Our little girl is growing up"), rather than over-reaction (e.g., "Doesn't she like us anymore?"). But the latter is a predictable response to entering uncharted and unwelcome waters.

In case my repeatedly mentioning the challenges of adolescence has you feeling increasingly uneasy, let me digress briefly at this point to assure you that adolescence and disaster are not synonymous terms. Although some teenagers exhibit rather severe acting out behaviors, the vast majority navigate the teen years without major trauma. To say adolescence is relatively problem-free, however, is not to suggest that it is uneventful. Every "normal" adolescent is affected by the combination of physical, social, emotional and cognitive changes that are inherent in adolescent development. These changes promote autonomy and independence, necessary components of maturation. They also necessitate changes in family relationships and interaction.

When children believe parents are over-reacting, the parent-child relationship, as well as the specific issue (such as missing curfew), tends to deteriorate rather than improve. To illustrate, when I asked troubled teens about discipline, a consistent lament was that their rules became stricter as they became older. They felt that when they wanted to be *more* independent their parents tightened the reins. Based on the teens' remarks, there was an unquestionable pattern of their rules becoming stricter as their externalizing behaviors increased.

Ali described her situation in this way:

Ali:	[My parents] have admitted to me that they had really high expectations for me—I guess because when they adopted me they had this perfect image on how I was going to grow up. And once I started going off that path they just kept getting more and more strict, thinking that I'd learn. And I never did.
JAM:	So they kept adding more rules?
Ali:	Yep, to try to, like, break me down.

Rebecca called it "annoying" that her rules always changed. According to her, in seventh grade she could "listen to whatever music I wanted," but in eighth grade her mother threw all her compact disks away. She lamented, "She just totally changed and made it not many rules to a lot of rules."

Ali and Rebecca were among the teens who responded to stricter rules with obstinacy and disobedience. Mike's comment regarding rules was representative of the others. He said simply, "[The rules] didn't bother me 'cause I didn't obey them."

So, what's a parent to do? Surely they can't be faulted for stiffening the rules as their child's behavior deteriorates. Once again, simple solutions don't exist. But we do know that parents need to set the pattern early and continue to discipline their children with composure, warmth, firmness, and wisdom.

Both the *parent* and the *child* need to understand that (a) the rules and expectations will likely be adjusted (whether they become more or less lenient) as the child's behavior changes; and (b) the parent remains the ultimate authority until the child becomes self-sufficient and independent of the family in which s/he was raised.

Remember the principle of promoting self-regulation? Discipline isn't just about calming today's turbulent waters and avoiding icebergs. It's attempting to ensure that our children are eventually capable of steering their own boat.

Family Meetings

Previously we discussed various parenting styles. The authoritarian approach, which is heavy on control with little warmth, tends to result in belligerence, dependency, and insecurity. One of the missing components in the authoritarian approach is communication. "Because I said so" is deemed by the parent as a sufficient reason to enforce rules; no explanation is offered or considered necessary. The problem with this approach isn't so much that parents are making the decisions; that's generally as it should be. However, when parents are seen as unyielding and insensitive autocrats, we are inviting our children to question, protest, and even rebel.

Family meetings are a way to promote communication, understanding and a sense of respect among family members.

Simply put, they are an opportunity for each family member to listen and to be heard on any topic he or she believes to be important. These family times can include fun topics (e.g., deciding where the family will go for Sunday's picnic), practical issues (e.g., who's taking Sara to gymnastics tomorrow), as well as ample time to discuss, establish and revisit the set of rules by which the family lives. Obviously, these meetings need to be designed to fit each individual family and the content needs to be altered as children get older and family needs and dynamics change. A child of three may have little to contribute but at 13 may have a whole lot to say. But the basic rules that govern these family times can remain fairly simple and consistent. For example, (a) All family members will be present. (b) Anything can be shared, as long as it is stated in a respectful and appropriate manner. (c) Each person has a right to speak without interruption or ridicule. (d) Each person's input will be considered and valued. (e) With everyone's opinions and needs carefully and sensitively weighed, the ultimate decision rests with the parents.

I've presented the concept of family meetings in a very simplistic way. But, rather than offering a precise model, my purpose is to motivate you to consider initiating regular family meetings in your home. If suited to your family dynamics, individual temperaments, and diverse needs, this forum can play a valuable role in promoting healthy interaction and connectedness. Additionally, you are establishing a potentially meaningful and useful precedent as your family grows and changes.

* * * * *

The following checklist may guide you as you attempt to evaluate your discipline practices:

- When disciplining my child, does my discipline more accurately reflect my child's actual behavior that I am attempting to correct or my own mood, circumstances or stress level?

- When disciplining my child, do I consider the "big picture"—the person my child will some day become—rather than short term convenience or ease?

- When committed to a particular ideology because I believe it to be best for my child, do I waver based on what other parents allow their children to do?

- Do I really believe that discipline is *good* for my child? If so, do my words and behaviors demonstrate this belief?

- Do I allow my child to control our household by acquiescing to his/her continual wants and demands? (Note: Because it is so difficult for us to see ourselves as we really are, perhaps a very trusted friend can help you answer this question.)

- Is my discipline characterized by a balanced combination of warmth and control? If not, do I feel it should be?

- Do I maintain my composure rather than disciplining my child in anger?
- Do I get "hung up" on relatively insignificant behaviors or do I attempt to distinguish the truly important from the relatively unimportant?
- Do my discipline strategies suggest I understand the difference between childish irresponsibility and willful defiance?
- Am I training my child to listen, follow instructions, and assume responsibility for his/her behaviors?

* * * * *

A ship safely reaches its intended destination under the watchful eye of its captain, who must make certain all crew members understand and abide by the rules of the sea. The captain knows well what is required for safe navigation and realizes that poor decisions, on the part of any one of the ship's crew, can lead to calamity. The crew may not always appreciate the standards by which they are expected to adhere. Nevertheless, the captain undauntedly stays the course. Are you, as captain of your family's ship, providing the calm, firm and goal-oriented direction that your children need?

Eight
A TRUSTWORTHY COMPASS

We cannot direct the wind, but we can adjust the sails.

- Bertha Calloway[1]

In an often quoted Scripture verse, the writer of Proverbs urges parents to "Train a child in the way he should go."[2] The word "train" suggests to me that there is more to raising children than the *laissez faire* belief that babies arrive on the scene pre-programmed and, thus, parents should simply stay out of the way and "let nature take its course." This hands-off approach stresses heredity over any environmental influences; therefore, parents are only accountable for their child's behaviors to the degree that they are responsible for their genetic make-up. Adherence to this viewpoint relieves parents of any liability should things go wrong or, for that matter, any credit should things go right. In fact, the *laissez faire* philosophy makes a book such as this totally unnecessary and its purported ideas quite absurd. But I see things otherwise. I believe that leaving our children's training to chance is no less absurd than attempting to navigate without a trustworthy compass or allowing the wind to carry us at will.

If you're still reading, I assume you give at least partial

mental assent to the proverb about training with which I began this chapter. Training a child "in the way he should go" is consistent with setting goals for our children and making plans to achieve them, as discussed earlier. However, to complement the planning that's done in advance, we as parents also need to make the most of opportunities along the way.

Teachable Moments

Parent-child shared daily activities and routine chores provide innumerable teaching opportunities. These moments occur naturally, assuming two components are present: (a) the parent and child are together, and (b) the parent is tuned in and turned on to the child's world. The first point regarding togetherness is obvious, I know. But it's an important reminder that we cannot possibly take advantage of teachable moments, by their very nature spontaneous, when we are not with our children. The second point, being tuned in to our children and effective parenting practices, has the potential of turning any time with our children into an invaluable opportunity. A teachable moment may present itself at the shopping mall, when a child spies an action figure he desperately wants. He can't buy it because he exhausted his cash reserve last week on an impulsive purchase of a fancy-looking but cheaply-made toy truck that is already in the trash. A parent who responds to the child's plea with a patient, logical and gentle explanation, thus assisting the child to make the connection between his past actions and current dilemma, is taking advantage of a teachable moment. A parent who appeases him by giving him money to purchase the action figure, is not.

Responsibility

"With privilege, goes responsibility" is a phrase I remember using often when our children were young. Without much stretch of the imagination, I am sure you can think of many fitting occasions to pass along this friendly reminder to your offspring.

An important component of training is providing our children with experiences that will encourage them to become responsible. Parents can fall into several different categories in this particular aspect of training. Some parents, possibly those who feel they were robbed of their own childhood by too much responsibility too soon, want to shield their own children from any potential unpleasantness, including effort and self-discipline that accompany productivity. These parents allow their children to do only what they choose to do. Other parents find it's much easier to simply do what needs to be done themselves, rather than face the hassle of prodding resistant children. Still others fail to see the value of purposely teaching children to be responsible. Once again, as we consider the most effective way to parent, let's step back and look at the big picture: the persons our children will someday become.

A four-year-old can easily be taught to set the dinner table. If he willingly agrees that this will be his contribution to dinner ("with privilege, goes responsibility"—he plans to eat), initially it is likely to be fun to him and endearing to the parent— to say nothing of how pleased grandma will be when she comes to visit. But the first few days, before the novelty wears off, is only the precursor to actual training. Training begins when it's no longer a game that the child plays for his own amusement. If he refuses to willingly assume the responsibility of regularly setting the table, we as parents are faced with a choice. We set the table ourselves, enlist someone else who will willingly oblige, or insist that he do it. The first two choices are much simpler in the short-term: table set quickly and efficiently, no hassle, everyone's at least relatively happy. However, in keeping with our commitment to look beyond the moment and think long-term, the third choice, in spite of its potential for discord and grief, is a far superior option. Not insisting that children fulfill their responsibilities is a wide open invitation to rebel against future parental injunctions.

A few very simple guidelines can assist us in our efforts to train our children to become responsible. First, our expectations must be realistic, suited to our children's still-developing cognitive and fine motor skills. No amount of instruction can equip young children to safely handle the antique fruit bowl that has been in the family for five generations but they are very capable of putting out the placemats and napkins.

Remember that training is a process that takes time and effort. Rather than assuming our children can read our minds, we need to explicitly explain, maybe several times, what we want them to do and how they are to do it. If we give our children hurried, non-specific instructions (e.g., "Set the table"), it is likely that our expectations will not be met. Worse yet, if we then admonish our children for not doing it "correctly" and proceed to rearrange the flatware or refold the napkins, we are sending them the message that their efforts are inferior.

Another guideline in effectively training our children and enhancing their perception of work is giving them choices, whenever possible and as appropriate. If their responsibility is to assist in setting the dinner table, they can choose to put out either the plates and glasses or the spoons and forks. This will give them a sense of empowerment and the intended purpose is still achieved: they are being taught to be responsible.

A final rule of thumb that minimizes potential distress, particularly for the parent, pertains to the outcome of the tasks children are asked to do. In the spirit of fostering creativity, we may want to give children some latitude regarding how the table is set. This is a good idea, assuming we can live with their decision to replace the freshly cut floral centerpiece with a Lego fort and toy soldiers.

Serving Others

The purpose of this brief section is to remind us of something I believe to be an essential and frequently overlooked component of child training: teaching our children to serve. Whether we like it or not, our children are growing up in an "it's-all-about-me" world. To counteract countless alluring invitations for self-gratification, we must conscientiously identify opportunities for our children to serve rather than to be served. This requires one commodity of which young parents never seem to have enough: *time*. But in order for our children to grow up to be sensitive to the cares and needs of others and to truly understand what it means to put others before themselves, opportunities for them to serve should be deliberately planned. We teach them the spirit and joy of serving not only by modeling it in our own lives (e.g., by caring for the neighbor's children so the exhausted mother can get a much-needed break from the daily routine) but directly involving them in service (e.g., by making small gifts for the residents of a local nursing facility and personally delivering them). By conscientiously incorporating service to others in your family's busy routine, you will be undermining the world's message and human nature's tendency to focus on me and mine.

Respect

Previously, we discussed parents' treating their children

with a lack of respect. Now, in the context of discipline, we will move on to a complementary phenomenon. In the past couple of decades I have observed a huge tendency for children, particularly when they reach pre-adolescent age, to treat their parents (and other elders) with disrespect. Is there a connection between the way children are treated by adults and the way they treat adults? No doubt. But I speculate that parents' treating their children disrespectfully is only part of the problem. I believe that today's parents often fail to command respect as they should.

Command respect? That seems harsh for the 21st century, doesn't it? After all, unlike previous generations, we are attuned to the importance of parenting with sensitivity, warmth and compassion, and we certainly do not want our children to fear us. But I use the term "command" advisedly and with conviction. For whatever reason, parents have become increasingly unable or unwilling to establish positions of authority in their children's lives. Children learn to use nagging and whining effectively and exhausted parents give in just to get some peace and quiet. Manipulative and coercive behaviors that are reinforced by parental compliance become powerful tools in an adolescent's arsenal.

The increased tendency for children to disregard authority figures extends beyond the home and affects other contexts, such as the school, as well. Over the years that I attended our sons' junior high open houses and sat in on their classes, I saw a pattern of deterioration of students' respect for their teachers, exhibited by talking without permission, interrupting and a general disregard for the teacher's efforts to teach. I was, frankly, quite appalled by the students' apparent ability and eagerness to take advantage of weak and thus ineffective classroom management. Rather than its intended purpose, the classroom was providing opportunities for youth to hone the skills of exploitation, rudeness and disrespect.

My increasing concerns regarding children's attitudes toward authoritative figures were reinforced and confirmed as I talked with troubled teens. Perhaps Sara best summed up the prevailing attitude among the respondents: "I wanted to do what I wanted to do. And so I didn't want someone telling me that I couldn't do something . . . . I was definitely stuck on not letting [my parents] know anything about me."

Several of the teens expressed disrespect not only for their parents but for other authority figures as well. Singled out were persons associated with law enforcement. This was how one 15-year-old explained it:

George:	I hate cops. It's always been my attitude.
JAM:	Why do you think that was the case?
George:	I think it was mainly that I didn't like authority.

Ali, who admired her friends who were fearless, said she ran from the police the first couple of times they came to the house. But, she explained, "[If I was] in the jail or the sheriff's office . . . they'd just sit me down and talk to me or my brother and I would just sit there and just pretty much laugh at what they had to say." Steve believed that the police stopped and searched him for no legitimate reason, but rather simply because he dressed "punk" and rode a skateboard. In his words, "That made me form an opinion about authority, at least the ones that I was confronted by, that I just didn't like them. So I showed it to them some of the time."

A few of the teens had no respect for anyone in authority. When I asked Mike about authority, he had a ready answer.

Mike:	Uh, screw it. I didn't have any authority. So I didn't have to obey authority.
JAM:	Who did you consider "authority"?
Mike:	Teachers, principals, parents, people at church. I think basically anyone that had given me an order and I was supposed to obey it.
JAM:	And you were not responsive, respectful of that authority?
Mike:	Course not. I wouldn't do anything; I'd just walk away.

Ali said, "I didn't have any respect for any authority, you know what I mean?"

Very few children joyfully submit to authority, as it always seems to run counter to human nature. Nevertheless, orderly, well-balanced, and productive lives are not feasible in its absence.

Morals and Beliefs

As has been evident throughout this book, my philosophical convictions include the tenets of the Christian faith, based on Biblical principles. The discussion that follows will primarily appeal to those of you who share, or at least tolerate, those convictions.

Training in the realm of morals and beliefs is both indirect and direct. We talked previously about the critical importance of modeling the behaviors we desire for our children. According to a well-known child psychologist, "Values are caught, not taught."[3] The sense of this statement seems to parallel the adage "What you do speaks so loud, I can't hear what you're saying." Talking to our children about moral standards and their underlying belief system is relatively worthless if our words and behaviors communicate a message to the contrary. The ideal, then, is combining a consistent message of verbal teaching and modeling.

Parents, the Bible says that it is our task to pass our

faith along to our children. Note the following verse: "[God] commanded our forefathers to teach their children, so the next generation would ... put their trust in God and would not forget his deeds but would keep his commands."[4]

Children can be taught from a very early age that the Bible is more than just another storybook. They can have a Bible of their own, with text and pictures appropriate for their ages. Because it provides a guide for life, the Bible's authority and usefulness for instruction can very naturally be incorporated into daily living. When our elementary-aged children struggled with integrity, rather than just telling them that lying was wrong we would ask them to get their Bible. We would then sit down with them, help them locate Exodus 20:6 and have them read what God had to say on the topic of lying: "You must not lie." This wasn't in any way meant to be a heavy-handed tactic to "put the fear of God" into our children, making Him look like an oppressive dictator waiting to pounce when his subjects disappoint Him. Rather, it was intended to help them understand that there's a reliable, clearly outlined guide to help them distinguish right from wrong whether or not we are around to remind them. We also hoped to impress our children with the desirability of looking to the highest and ultimate authority as a source of direction, comfort and meaning.

Beyond the Bible itself, there are many Christian books that can have powerful and far-reaching impact in young children's lives. A favorite at our house, and a bedtime ritual for many years, was the ever-popular story of *The Chronicles of Narnia*.[5] My husband read the complete *Chronicles of Narnia* to the children several times before they began reading them on their own. The last time I heard the *Chronicles* mentioned, one of our grown sons was reading them to his own children, and the other was reading them with his girlfriend.

In addition to books, music can play a very powerful role in training young children. Our sons learned many, many Bible stories and Biblical principles through the medium of music. Once, when one of our sons was three and was listening to a music tape, a song began playing that he recognized. He called from his room: "Mommy, I hear a song we sing at church. I wuv it; I just wuv it."

To this day, lyrics from songs to which my children listened when they were very young frequently come to mind and I find them not just nostalgic, but instructive. My husband can no doubt relate to this, as music was a part of our sons' childhood that we all shared. How could we miss the point of lyrics such as "Be patient, be patient, don't be in such a hurry. If you are impatient, you only start to worry,"[6] and "Kids under construction, maybe the paint is still wet. Kids under construction, the Lord may not be finished yet."[7]

I believe that Christianity is a way of life prompted by personal conviction, not simply a set of rituals by which we must abide. That being said, there are many natural outgrowths of Christian beliefs that involve customs, practices and routines—rituals, if you will. High on the list of importance in my mind is prayer. We can pray for our children when they are still in the womb, once they're in our arms, at the side of their cradles and then by their cribs. We can pray not only for them, but with them. If prayer is a natural, instinctual part of our lives, it is likely to become a part of theirs as well.

Prayer, no matter how simplistic its delivery, is talking with God. Through young children's meal-time prayers they are learning to be grateful to God for providing their basic needs. Our son's family sings and signs the following meal time prayer: "The Lord's been good to me. And so I thank the Lord, for giving me the things I need—the sun and the rain and the apple seed. The Lord's been good to me."[8] When they tell God they're sorry for hitting someone, they begin to understand the concept of a forgiving God who cares about their choices and actions. And, when they ask God to help them not to be afraid of the dark, they begin to see Him as a source of protection and comfort.

Attending church is another ritual that our children learn from us. I have frequently observed families for whom sports, sleeping in, and even "family time," take precedent over going to church. I am not saying that occasionally missing church is inexcusable. But I do want to gently remind you that when other things consistently take priority over going to church or church-related activities, we are sending a clear message to our children about church's relative unimportance. One reason I feel it is so important to establish the church-going pattern early is because of what I've observed during many years as a youth group sponsor. When young children become adolescents and parents become increasingly aware of potentially negative peer influences, they often look to the church youth program for help. But, if church attendance hasn't been a priority up to this point, the child continues to view it as optional, and parents have little leverage for convincing their child otherwise.

One final note before we leave the topic of church attendance. This actually probably goes without saying, but I will make no assumptions here. Your young children should never, ever hear you grumble about the length of the sermon, the type of music, or anything else related to the pastors, the church, or its attendees. By succumbing to the temptation to voice dissatisfaction, parents seriously undermine the very principles they should be modeling.

* * * * *

As you attempt to train your children in the way they should go, perhaps the following self-check will help guide you.

- Do I spend ample time with my children to take advantage of teachable moments?
- Do I miss teachable moments because I am engrossed in

my own agenda rather than tuned in to my children's world?

- Are my expectations of my child realistic?
- Do I provide my children with opportunities to become responsible or do I tend to spare them from things that aren't easy or fun?
- Are my children respectful of me and other adults?
- Do I consistently teach and model the values by which I expect my children to live?
- Do my behaviors indicate that I believe reading the Bible and praying are important?
- Do I model positive behaviors toward the church and fellow parishioners, including regular attendance and no gossip or negative comments?

* * * * *

A captain depends on buoys to warn of potential danger and mark the path his ship can safely navigate. Similarly, the beliefs and values parents pass along to their children serve to guide them through unknown and dangerous waters and keep them headed in the right direction.

Nine
CREATING A SAFE HARBOR

No culture has ever been able to provide a better shipyard
for building storm-proof vessels for the journey of man
from the cradle to the grave than the individual
nourished in a loving family.

- Laurens van der Post & Jane Taylor[1]

Our 13-year-old son rushed in the back door, took a deep breath, and exclaimed, "I'm so glad to be here. It's like rounding third base and heading toward home. I know I'm finally going to be safe." The school bus ride had been particularly unsettling for a sensitive young man. Two older students in the back of the bus were unabashedly rolling "joints" and our son's sense of security was shaken. He had run as fast as he could from the bus stop to our back door and arrived breathlessly; I was waiting with a hug, a snack and a listening ear. He had reached a safe harbor.

One of the greatest gifts we can give our children is a sanctuary—a place of security and protection. Much as God is "a shield for all who take refuge in Him,"[2] our responsibility as parents is to provide security for our children who look to us for refuge. Anthropologist Margaret Mead is quoted as saying, "One of the oldest human needs is having someone wonder where you are when you don't come home at night."[3] Inherent in this statement is the sense that someone truly cares for you.

Research findings consistently indicate that a sheltering home environment not only enhances children's early development but lessens the probability that, when they reach the adolescent years, they will make poor decisions regarding risky behaviors such as alcohol and drug use.[4] I was struck by the apparent absence of a haven for many teens who were living in a residential facility because of their own antisocial behaviors and the ensuing family conflict. They appeared sad as they expressed their perceptions of their families and homes. Ali said that she had felt isolated and described herself as "looking for someone to go to when I had problems . . . someone who'd care about me and care what would happen to me." Likewise, Mindy's comments were poignant: "I knew that I didn't have anyone in the world—like my family, my whole family . . . has a lot of problems and I knew that there was no one for me there, like I had no family member that I could turn to." Sara spoke of the "terrible communication" within her home, and added, "at times I could never really tell if they loved me. So it's kind of like I needed to go somewhere else to find that . . ." Faith's family epitomized a home that was anything but a refuge. Her single-parent family was "led" by a drug-addicted mother who would tell the children she was going to the grocery store and not come home for several days. Faith, as the oldest child, assumed responsibility for her younger siblings. Clearly, linked to the teens' perceived lack of support and love was a search to find someone to fill that void.

The time to cultivate an atmosphere that will continue to draw your children in, rather than push them away, is while they are young. Take a moment to reflect on these questions. What is it like, through a child's eyes of innocence and dependence, to be a part of your family? Have you taken time to carefully evaluate your home and ensure that what happens there is not left to chance? Let's discuss a few specific components of the home environment that affect children's sense of self, belonging and security.

Traveling at How Many Knots?

If your home is characterized by what might be described as a "morning rush hour," think for a moment about what your children might say if they could identify and articulate their feelings. Would it possibly be something like: "Why can't we ever stop and play at the park?" "Why don't I ever have time to pick my bits of alphabet cereal out of my bowl one by one and see if we can make some words?" "Why do you always say 'hurry, hurry, hurry'?"

Rushing, in the morning or at any other time, is contrary

to children's nature. Although adults sometimes assume children have limitless adaptability, they are actually very susceptible to stress. When children fail to respond during a barrage of parental commands such as "Get your shoes on NOW!" and "If you don't come NOW I'm going to leave without you!" (an inappropriate as well as empty threat), they are attempting to gain some control over circumstances that go against the core of their beings. I often remind parents that attempting to rush preschoolers by telling them they're going to be late is a total exercise in futility. Due to limited cognitive ability, preschoolers' thinking is characterized by self-absorption. Practically, this means that nothing starts until they have arrived; therefore, it is not possible for them to be late.

Hurrying has permeated many aspects of today's family life. In part, the current trend to register young children in activities—ballet, tumbling, swimming, T-ball, piano—is responsible for the unfortunate combination of snack foods and cat naps in the back seat of a mini-van. Sooner is not necessarily better when it comes to enrolling children in structured activities. Particularly poor choices are activities that do not suit a child's schedule or inflict pressure to achieve beyond his or her capabilities. By contrast, parent-child picnics at the park, trips to the library, baking and delivering cookies to a house-bound elderly friend, and playing catch in the backyard can be arranged around the family schedule, enjoyed at a leisurely pace, and individually suited to children's aptitude, interests and stamina.

A notable phrase among persons in the field of child development is "Play is a child's work." Optimum development unfolds naturally in the context of a carefree, stimulating environment that encourages exploring, choosing, initiating, creating, exercising, imagining . . . and simply being a child. Free play in small, informal groups provides opportunities for interaction, cooperation, sharing and communication under a parent's watchful eye and establishes the foundation for the formation of future relationships.

On a related point, we put much emphasis on early social interaction and adult-initiated cognitive stimulation, and rightly so. But rarely do we discuss the importance of young children being allowed solitary time. When a 7-month-old is observing the cause and effect of grasping and shaking a chain of colorful plastic letters, we do not need to always "seize the moment" to talk about colors and the letters of the alphabet. When a toddler is happily engaged with building nothing in particular out of blocks, it is not necessary that we intervene at that moment to demonstrate how to build a house. When a 7-year-old is constructing a "science experiment" out of straws, sand, rubber bands, and discarded margarine containers, we do not need to interrupt his thoughts to interject our good ideas. As an aside, think about whether it's sometimes possible that when parents force their way into their children's world it's a reflection of their own, rather than their child's, needs. A mother who needs to feel needed, or a father who equates being alone with loneliness, is much less likely to allow a child time to experience the wonder of independent exploration and discovery. Young children's abilities are being stretched as they examine, contemplate, and manipulate on their own. And it's so important to remember that, whether a young child is experimenting with black and purple finger paint or making snowmen out of marshmallows, *the process is more important than the product.* Through solitary play, young children learn to think, function, and make independent decisions. They also learn that being alone can be more than tolerable or acceptable; it can be fun. Why do I feel this is noteworthy? Early patterns form the basis for future attitudes and conduct. Contentment with being alone, independent decision-making, and self-sufficiency can be vital survival traits during the adolescent years.

If you find yourself continually rushing your child, as well as yourself, from one activity, errand or event to another, you are not alone. Consider how many conferences, regardless of their primary focus, include workshops on stress and time management. We are part of a rat race culture, and our children are bearing the brunt of much of the pressure we put on ourselves and pass along to them. It is counter-productive to allow children to experience pressures at an early age in an attempt to "prepare them for the future." They will inevitably face the demands of life in the 21st century soon enough.

Wants vs. Needs

A major shift in the pace of American families is the result of a societal movement over the past several decades. Forty years ago, the vast majority of families had a full-time, stay-at-home parent. By contrast, at the beginning of the 21st century both parents were employed in 63 percent of two-parent families with children under eighteen.[5] For some, the decision is based on the parent's making a deliberate choice between a career path and staying at home. For others, dual incomes are a perceived necessity, as managing on one income has become increasingly difficult due to the rising cost of living. If you fall into either category—choosing to work or feeling you have no choice, consider whether you could put a career on hold or manage with less income during your child's early years. For some homes one paycheck is simply insufficient to provide the family's basic needs, and, unfortunately, those parents truly have no viable option other than dual employment. Likewise, for a growing number of single parents, full-time employment is a necessity. However, for many parents, living on one income *can* be done. These are the parents to whom these next few paragraphs are directed.

Let's step back for a moment and access "sufficient" family

income in the context of today's culture. Whether it pertains to cars, homes, vacations, electronic toys, or all of the above, "bigger and better" has permeated American society. The accumulation of stuff is consciously and subconsciously affecting our thinking and driving our decisions. Many parental pairs believe that they must both be employed in order to give their children "the best." Rather than defining what's best in terms of the accumulation of possessions, we must view it in terms of the quality of our present family life and the groundwork we are laying for future relationships with our children.

When my husband and I were young parents, an elderly preacher's visit to our church was most timely. We have never forgotten his wise and insightful statement on that Sunday morning more than three decades ago. His seven words were these: "Richness consists of your fewness of wants." At that juncture of our life, my husband's income was sufficient to meet the needs of a family of three, but frugality was a necessity. My husband and I learned a lot about ourselves, possessions and priorities during the first few years of our marriage. I was particularly grateful that through my own upbringing I had learned the "waste not, want not" principle and the value of hard work. Both of these lessons have served me well throughout my life.

* * * * *

Take a moment to contemplate the following questions regarding the pace and priorities in your home.

- How would I define the overall tempo of our family life? Are we strolling at a pace that allows us to enjoy what is going on around us or charging through life? How often do I use the word "hurry"? How often am I stressed as a result of time pressure?

- Am I pleased with the pace of my life? Does it fit the physical and emotional needs of me and my children? Do I notice what is going on around me?

- If I am rushing, what are the causes? Too many parental commitments? Too many children's activities? Both?

- When I enroll my child in an activity, is it for myself or for my child? (Do I take pride in telling others that my 3-year-old is in gymnastics? Do I believe that somehow reflects positively on my parenting?)

- Before I make a work-related or volunteer commitment, do I carefully consider its impact on myself and my children?

- Do my spouse and/or I need to cut back on the time and energy we devote to employment? Have we honestly assessed our family's needs vs. our wants?

- Are there any pragmatic, deliberate changes I need to make so that my home and family life are more comfortably paced?

- If changes are needed, am I willing to make them?

*****

Before I leave this topic, I want to remind you that the hours, the days, the weeks, the months, and even the years, are very quickly here and gone. There's never a second chance to experience them. Listen to and trust the voice of a mother whose children are grown--someday you will look back and wonder where those priceless childhood years have gone. You will ask yourself whether you took the time to fully appreciate and enjoy each stage of life as much as you could have—and should have. I often think of the lyrics of the song, popular many years, called "Turn Around." The final stanza plaintively asks, "Where have they gone, our little ones, little ones/Where have they gone, our children our own?/Turn around and they're young, turn around and they're old/Turn around and they've gone and we've no one to hold."[6] For the sake of your children, as well as yourself, don't wait until tomorrow to slow down and truly cherish the fast-fleeting moments of childhood.

Routines and Rituals

In giving instructions to church leadership, the Apostle Paul wrote, ". . . everything should be done in an . . . orderly way."[7] This advice is well taken not just for churches, but for homes as well—especially those that include young children. Predictability breeds security and promotes well-being and children's biological and emotional internal clocks function best with regular routines.

Regularity involves not only *when* a particular routine will take place, but also *who* will participate and *what* will occur. Family mealtimes, which provide natural opportunities for cohesion, don't just happen. Particularly as children get older, merely getting all members to the table simultaneously can be difficult. Beyond physical togetherness, mealtimes can serve as an energizing and restoring touch point—a time for children and parents to share their day's delights and concerns in a caring, safe atmosphere, free of criticizing, arguing, and reprimanding. Mealtimes should be happy, conducive to enjoyment of the company as well as the food. (Have you ever wondered why in some homes singing at the table is not permissible? Doesn't it seem that it might be more appropriate for singing to be *required*?) As another example, regardless of what has transpired during the day, a one-on-one, peaceful bedtime routine—a short story, a song and a prayer—can serve as a balm and promote bonding between parent and child. Daily routines offer unlimited opportunities for family members to share significant moments in time.

Through rituals and routines, parents have the privilege of defining and designing the meaning of being a member of a particular family. As young children become preadolescents and begin moving in circles beyond the family, memories of traditions and celebrations sustain feelings of belonging. In addition to regular routines, activities such as summer vacations on the beach, 4th of July fireworks, Thanksgiving food baskets for a family in need, Christmas eve candlelight services and New Year's day brunches all serve to promote warmth, familiarity and connectedness among family members.

Birthday celebrations are a great opportunity to honor individual family members. The "birthday boy" or "birthday girl" (even if an adult) should feel especially loved and appreciated. Along with fun surprises that include the honoree's favorites, traditions that everyone shares enhance a family's feelings of unity and oneness. As an example, our family has carried on a tradition that began several generations ago. Commemorating birthdays includes singing three verses of happy birthday (two of which I've never heard elsewhere) and eating white nut cake with Aunt Dorothy's icing. A person, new to our family by marriage, was recently at his first family party. After hearing us discuss the cake, he innocently asked, "Have I met Aunt Dorothy?" No, he hadn't. And at that point we all realized that *none* of us, other than our mother, has any recollection of her. What we do know is that she made delicious icing and, more importantly, provided our family with a unique birthday tradition.

Perhaps you are wondering why I have spent several paragraphs stating the obvious. Doesn't everyone know that the family should eat meals together and children should feel special on their birthdays? First, there is a vast difference between knowing something intellectually and being sufficiently convinced of its importance to put it into practice. We need to be reminded that routines, shared activities, rituals, intentional family patterns and traditions—by *any* name— require thoughtfulness, planning, and priority status. Second, chances are I would not view this topic as nearly as significant had it not emerged as a glaring missing ingredient in the homes of the teens who participated in my research. Tonya, for example, described her family as "distant" and added, "We never really did a family activity or anything like that." According to Rebecca, her family didn't interact at all. Family meals were non-existent; she'd go to the kitchen to get her food and then eat in her room while talking on the phone to friends. Sara said that birthdays "really stand out" because those were the *only* times—a total of four times a year—the family ate dinner and played games together. When Rebecca and I were discussing family routines, she responded in a comical fashion, consistent with her quick wit. I asked, "Did you have any family routines or rituals that you remember?" to which she replied, "Uh, we usually end up yelling at each other at least once a night, but other than that not really."

As strongly as I have just defended the cause of family rituals, I would be remiss if I didn't add a caveat. I caution you to not force an activity on your family simply for the sake of routine, because a friend told you how much her family likes it, or because you remember enjoying it when you were a child. If something's not working, let it go. In addition, don't adhere to rituals or traditions so dogmatically that you lose your sense of perspective. If you, mom and dad, have the opportunity to take a Caribbean cruise, don't decline because someone else (or maybe even no one) would be reading your children's bedtime story for seven days. Traditions and routines without flexibility are hard to distinguish from hard-nosed, legalistic demands, which eventually chase children away rather than draw them in.

Having Fun

When one of our sons was in third grade, his teacher gave his class the following assignment: "What is your favorite place? Write about it." Our son's response was brief and to the point: "I like to be at home. It's fun there and it's always welcoming." When I recently pulled the weathered notebook page from my memorabilia file, I took a moment to reflect on those penciled words of some 18 years ago. The teacher's smiley face at the top of the page was no match for my own. I'm sure he didn't always view being at home as quite so desirable, but at least on that particular day my son answered the question the way I would have hoped.

What makes home a child's favorite place? At least in

part, I believe it's the ambience—how a home "feels." Balloons for no particular reason, walking barefoot in the rain, a book of Calvin and Hobbes on the coffee table, singing while doing dishes, sitting on the porch swing, blowing soap bubbles, picking a sprig of wild flowers, welcome home hugs, lively mealtime conversations, and, most certainly, laughter. A joyful home atmosphere promotes inner health and provides a haven and healing for the wounded, for, after all, "A cheerful heart is good medicine . . ."[8]

Part of the art of family fun is learning to enjoy the little, spontaneous moments of life, laughing together—and at oneself. "Inside" humorous stories occur naturally over time and bind family members' lives on a level none other share, thus reinforcing a sense of unity and belonging. I suggest keeping a journal, or just a spiral notebook, convenient at all times, for the express purpose of recording family humor. Statements such as "It's hundering, it's hundering," "Shuck up," "Shoot fire, I've got to go to bed," and "Oh, kids, here they start" mean nothing to you. But for our family, they bring back fun memories the four of us shared many years ago.

Sadly, many of the teens with whom I spoke had no memories of their homes being happy and fun. In fact, it seemed to be quite the opposite. Sara said it succinctly: "I just didn't like being home because it wasn't a happy place." She admitted that she spent time at friends' homes to get away from her own.

Ali described her dad and brother as "people I didn't want to be around" and added, "It just made me want to leave, and so I did." How very sad when children leave home because they dislike their homes and the people who live there.

Even children who enjoy their families begin to spend less time at home and more time with their peers as they near adolescence. This is as it should be; it's part of growing up and is consistent with the new level of social and emotional independence for which they are striving. I've heard it said that the best way to keep kids at home is to make sure your home is pleasant . . . and let the air out of their tires. Moving away from the familiar nest called home is normal, expected and desired. But when angry children storm or sneak out the back door as a means of escape, it is evident that they do not perceive their home as a refuge.

Time for Spouse and Self

Let's recap. Our homes should be fun-filled, orderly and stress-free havens in which our children can smile and grow. We, as parents, must selflessly throw our entire beings into making that ideal a reality. What a perfect plan . . . assuming that neither we nor our spouses have any needs of our own. Trying to be all things to all people all the time simply does not work out for mere mortals.

The home environment is less than optimal when the

needs of any family member, child or adult, are ignored. In two-parent homes, part of creating a positive home environment for our children is conscientiously cultivating the relationship between ourselves and our spouses. Let me speak specifically to mothers here, because that's a role to which I can relate. Putting our children's wants before those of our husband's is something to which many of us are prone. His needs may not be as obvious or seem as urgent as rocking a fussy baby or teaching a toddler to share her animal crackers. Nevertheless, we must remain aware of, and sensitive to, how easy it is for our children's needs to take precedent over our husband's. I truly believe this phenomenon is at least partially to blame for the high rate of divorce among couples with young children. Jointly raising young children tends to draw you together or drive you apart. I encourage you to intentionally strive for the former option.

Looking beyond the present, when the pitter-patter of little feet running down the hall is nothing but a distant memory, you and the person with whom you share the morning paper, the toothpaste tube, and the leftover casseroles, should still be intimately and emotionally embracing life together. Every day we make decisions (be they conscious or subconscious) of whether we will foster or neglect this relationship that forms the very foundation of our family.

Finally, you may have heard this definition of JOY: "Jesus first, Others second, and Yourself last." Generally, that's a good principle for Christian parenting, since God should be first in our lives and selflessness seems to be an essential quality to adequately fulfilling a parental role. However, if we as parents allow our emotional, physical, and spiritual resources to become totally depleted, we cannot even begin to create a healthy environment for the other members of our family. Sometimes we don't even realize that we're neglecting ourselves. In humility (and because I told you I'd be honest with you), I will share with you an example of this from my own life, many years ago, when I was a parent of young children. My husband asked me to do something for him—some simple little request, like getting him the car keys. I vividly recall my totally inappropriate response: "Okay, and when I finish that I'll become a doormat and you can walk on me." I can still remember the look of confusion on my husband's face. As for me, I felt utterly ashamed. We no doubt both were thinking "Where did *that* come from?" Although I was oblivious to my own psychological state, I was undoubtedly experiencing overload if such a small and reasonable request pushed me over the edge.

We simply must take time for renewal of our own bodies, souls and spirits in order to meet the needs of those we love. Throwing pebbles into a brook, soaking in a bubble bath, listening to soft music, having tea with a close friend, sensing God's presence through quiet time with Him—there are endless ways to be sure we aren't continually giving of ourselves without replenishing our inward resources. How comfortable would we be sailing on a ship whose captain consistently worked 18 hour days, leaving little time for physical renewal and no time at all for social and emotional support? Trying to give too much is unhealthy for us and for those about whom we care so much.

Ten
TURBULENT SEAS

It is better to meet danger than to wait for it.
He that is on a lee shore, and foresees a hurricane,
stands out to sea and encounters a storm to avoid a shipwreck.
- Charles Caleb Colton[1]

As captains of our families' vessels, we generally feel that we have some control over what happens onboard--that is, within the four walls of our homes. But all too soon we must begin to prepare our children for the turbulent seas, in the form of external forces, which our ship and its occupants will inevitably encounter. When our children are young, selecting and controlling the influences in their lives is relatively manageable. But negative societal forces, over which we have little or no control, begin to have an impact on our children's thoughts, attitudes, and behaviors at a very early age.

No 21st century parent needs to be told that countless forces threaten to disrupt America's families. Societal standards have deteriorated markedly over the past several decades and, when we no longer are able to monitor our children 24/7, we can safely assume that they will encounter a value system very unlike the one we have attempted to instill.

Who and what are these ominous adversaries of the family? First, let's look at a powerful force with which most families struggle on a daily basis: the media. This broad influence, which includes television, video games, the internet and movies, is capable of leaving a potentially devastating mark on the young. U.S. children spend a daily average of 4 hours and 40 minutes in front of a screen of some kind.[2] Considering just the quantity of children's engagement with electronic media, there is cause for concern. But what about quality? Their eyes, ears and brains are processing a myriad of messages from sources with far different objectives than the ones we have in mind for our children.

Media's Influence

Let's begin with a discussion of potential negative repercussions of media use that have nothing to do with content. For instance, children's habitual television and video use can lead to their becoming observers *of* life rather than participants *in* life. They expect the world to amuse and entertain them at a fast-moving and exhilarating pace. Sympathize with me for a moment with kindergarten teachers, who are charged with the awesome task of building a solid foundation for our children's formal education. They must feel at a disadvantage when they realize that their young television and video connoisseurs are accustomed to glitzy and mesmerizing graphics to assist them in learning that "dog" begins with "d." Beyond increasing children's expectations of learning delivered via entertainment, media use has an indirect negative impact on children's overall academic performance by robbing them of time for leisure reading and other self-directed cognitive stimulation.

Media entertainment can also become a substitute for family socialization. Chosen carefully and used sparingly, movies and television can be an acceptable family pastime. However, when family members are seated side-by-side with the television—rather than each other—as the focus, meaningful play, interaction, communication, and problem-solving are conspicuously absent. "Pass the popcorn," "What did he say?" "I'm thirsty," and a bit of simultaneous laughter may be the only emotional touch points in two hours of "family time." When this happens, building relationships is taking a back seat to being entertained.

Further concern about media use pertains to childhood obesity, which is rising at an alarming rate and has frightening ramifications for our children's future well-being. Multiple studies have linked child obesity and media consumption, simply because more and more children are choosing inactivity (other than pushing the buttons on the video or tv remote) rather than exercise. The incidence of Type II diabetes, which is associated with obesity, has quadrupled in the last two decades. As television, computer and video games promote a sedentary lifestyle, they are hazardous to our children's health in more ways than one. Cravings for electronic entertainment seem to become increasingly difficult to satiate as children get older.

In terms of the *content* of media experiences, let's next consider the stark reality of the detrimental influences to which our children are regularly being lured, such as television, video games and the internet. Perhaps you are thinking you have heard it all--and maybe you have. But please indulge me a few pages to share my perspective on this extremely concerning phenomenon.

Violence

Violence, which is especially damaging to children ages eight and under,[3] pervades the world of television. How traumatizing to young children, who are developmentally unable to distinguish between fantasy and reality, when they see and hear delightfully intriguing animated characters being choked, shot, stabbed and literally blown apart. And with few negative consequences for perpetrators, children view violence as an acceptable and maybe even amusing way to settle real life conflict.[4] Viewing countless acts of violence has been consistently shown to cause children to become desensitized, and therefore less sympathetic to victims of real life violence. It further increases their fears that they themselves will become victims.[5]

Yes, the jury is in. The debate has long been settled about the connection between viewing violence and (a) aggressive attitudes, values, and behaviors in children and (b) diminished empathy toward human suffering. Those who have carefully monitored the impact of television violence over the last several decades are convinced of its deadly force. One physician purports, "... if, hypothetically, television technology had never been developed, there would today be 10,000 fewer homicides each year in the United States, 70,000 fewer rapes, and 700,000 fewer injurious assaults."[6]

In terms of video violence, we have much less research than on television violence, simply because the video rage (if you will pardon the pun) is a fairly recent phenomenon and long-term effects can not yet be assessed. But preliminary studies indicate that the negative impact of video playing may be even greater than that of television, movies or music.[7] Perhaps the reason is painfully obvious. With video games, our children are not just being entertained by *watching* graphically played-out violence; through simulation, it's as if they are actually perpetrators of the crimes.

In World War II, six decades and many worlds ago, only 20% of soldiers could bring themselves to shoot rifles at the enemy when they first went into combat. They had engaged in many practices involving nonhuman targets, but when they were supposed to aim and shoot at real people their natural inhibitions kicked in. But today's first-time soldiers have been found to be very different: 90% of them are able to shoot at the enemy. Why? One of the most plausible explanations is that through simulation soldiers are now practicing to shoot at humans, rather than inanimate targets, thus breaking down their inhibitions. The military actually uses point-and-shoot video games very similar to those our children are playing in the malls, in the lobbies of movie theaters and in our living rooms. When a child plays an interactive video game, he is learning to perfect the same conditioned reflex skills as a soldier in training to learn to kill.[8]

On the topic of children's movies, I will warn you in advance that what I am about to say may not be very popular. You might choose to discount what I am saying by labeling me as old-fashioned, naïve and out of touch. But in order to be true to myself and my convictions, I must tell you that I believe that Disney movies—an American institution with all of its accompanying games, toys, costumes, lunch boxes, clothing labels, and stuffed animals—are primarily about expanding The Walt Disney Company's financial conglomerate and not about providing wholesome family entertainment. No one can deny the skill with which Disney producers have amassed millions of loyal followers, escorting them into an enchanting world of make-believe and magic. Just last night I saw a commercial promoting Disney's 50th anniversary and found myself experiencing a sense of nostalgia, as memories took me back to a world of charm, adventure and fairy tale endings. But I contend that we as a society are so enthralled by the aura of Mickey Mouse, Cinderella and Aladdin that we blindly accept, and even endorse, Disney's film offerings without carefully scrutinizing the messages they are sending.

Personally, I would be much more comfortable with Disney movies if they weren't marketed to young children. But I can scarcely endure to sit in a theater of young children while they watch their animated heroes encounter multiple traumatic and life-threatening events (accompanied by appropriately dramatic background crescendos). Children cover their eyes, cry, laugh nervously or simply remain quietly fixated on the big screen as their beloved Simba sinks to utter despair, having seen his father fall from a cliff to a violent death. Further magnifying Simba's anguish is his belief that he is responsible for his father's demise. Just because children respond "I know" to parental assurances that "This is just pretend" does not mean that their cognitive development is anywhere close to sophisticated enough to satisfactorily process and assimilate what their senses are taking in.

As for my attempt to understand why parents choose to take their children to movies such as *The Lion King*, I reason that they must have believed the movie would be child-appropriate because Disney promoted it as such. Do not be fooled into believing that Disney upper management has your child's emotional well-being as top priority. The next time you are tempted to "treat" your children to the latest Disney in-theater or home movie, consider instead packing a picnic and going to a nearby park, enjoying an excursion to the children's area of the local library, building a birdhouse, setting up a lemonade stand, playing catch, baking cookies or riding bikes and tricycles around the neighborhood.

I will end this discussion of television, movie and video violence with a pungent quote from a group of professionals, members of the American Academy of Pediatrics, who take our children's well-being very seriously: "The strength of the correlation between media violence and aggressive behavior is greater than the correlation between calcium intake and bone mass, or the correlation between lead ingestion and lower IQ."[9] If a quote such as this doesn't compel us to carefully monitor and restrict our children's intake of violence, I'm not sure what will.

Internet

A relatively new media phenomenon, whose incredibly extensive impact we are just beginning to comprehend, is the Internet. Like video games, the internet is an attractive, interactive, invigorating and potentially addictive medium. Younger and younger children are becoming adept at "dialing up" and using the internet for e-mailing, instant messaging, games, music, homework and even shopping. Perfectly suited to a hurry-up world that thrives on instant gratification and prefers the rush of superficial encounters over commitment, the internet provides immediate answers, instant entertainment and overnight delivery. But for all its convenience and potential for making our lives easier and more enjoyable, the Internet can lead children down a sinister path. One of the best discussions of this topic, in my opinion, comes from a book called *Parents Under Siege*.[10] Using the term "the dark side of life," the authors discuss the vulgarity and degradation that are but a mouse click away from our children's minds and hearts. In addition to pornography and other x-rated sites, chat rooms can be extremely dangerous, as they offer validation for children "filled with rage at the injustice of life" and "steeped in a sense of meaninglessness . . . . The dark side of the Internet magnifies, validates, and extends the dark side of the culture as it is shaped in music (from the absolute nihilism of rocker Marilyn Manson to the foul and hateful lyrics of some gangst[er] rap music), in movies and television (where the boundaries of the cruel and vicious seem to expand each year), and in video games, where all the nastiness comes together in a coherent whole."[11]

With just a click of the mouse, impressionable youth have access to instructions for building bombs; chat rooms that glorify and magnify the worst in the socially alienated, angry, and downtrodden; and adult-only sites replete with pornographic scenes and subject matter. The reality is that use of the internet is believed to have played a major role in several horrific events of the past decade. Take, for example, Kip Kinkel, the teenager who in a most calculated manner shot his father, mother and two classmates with guns he had obtained via the internet and kept hidden in the attic of his family's home. A combination of conflict with his father, poor academic performance, failed attempts at athletic endeavors and non-reciprocated romantic overtures seemed to drive him to seek the solitude and safety of his room. In an emotionally vulnerable state, the internet provided a non-threatening and accepting outlet for his fantasies and frustrations as well as validation of his penchant for violence and death.

In order to more fully understand the potential of the internet, and specifically of the power of assuming an on-line persona, I talked with several teens who navigate the internet as effortlessly as I drop a slice of bread into the toaster each morning. They understand the internet culture, where various fictitious names ("handles") can be assumed depending on the setting- -i.e., the forum, chat room or instant messaging conversation that one is entering. As they shed their identities and step into a world of make-believe, they are free to engage in stimulating conversation with no externally imposed accountability, boundaries, or consequences. Young adolescents, driven by the desire to appear mature and wise, are particularly vulnerable as they form an emotional connection with uninhibited strangers of unknown identity and character. We have heard far too many tragic stories of young victims falling prey to sexual predators whom they've "met" on line.

One mother of three teens described to me her great misgivings about her children's access to the internet. She said it was as if they had "unleashed a monster" in their home. So what are parents to do, short of placing each of our children in an impenetrable bubble?

Parents should invest in internet blocking software to minimize children's accidental or deliberate access to potentially harmful sites. Although blocking decreases the likelihood children will enter these sites, in reality no software guarantees complete protection. So, in addition, let's go back to three points we discussed earlier in the book, all pertaining to patterns formed in the early years. First, we need to closely monitor our children not only when they are amenable to our supervision but especially when they protest. Second, we must frequently and emphatically reiterate the family standards and expectations to which they are being held. Third, we should be ever mindful that the only real protection during the teen years is self-regulation--that is, the ability and will to make the right choices even when no one's looking. This is developed through pragmatic training that begins when children are very young.

Music

Music, in its various forms, has been a meaningful and powerful influence since the beginning of time. In today's world, perhaps more than in any other era, music has become a means of expressing ideologies and motivating actions. Music draws converts, if you will, to a particular way of viewing life. Equally important to its ideology is music's ability to provide a sense of identity and an accepting clique of fellow followers, a much sought-after commodity among America's youth. There are multiple examples of particular music "artists" and genres becoming a culture within a culture, as they permeate and dictate their groupies' thoughts, moods, speech, behaviors, mannerisms and belief system. The power of the medium of music should not be underestimated, as some of the teens involved in my research would testify.

George told me that rappers became his idols. He and his friends were drug dealers, not because they were "poor kids in the ghetto," but because of greed. "It's just like they say in rap," George told me. "Greed, money, sex . . . . They wouldn't rap about it if they didn't love it." Rebecca said that her "attitude started getting a lot worse" when she started listening to Eminem, known for his lyrics on hatred, rage, and violence. Sara likened the influence of music to that of peers because of its ability to get you "all worked up." She explained, "They're words and they're telling you something. Even if you're like,

'Oh, I just like the beat,' you're still hearing these words that can get you all excited about something like doing drugs or fighting or being, as they would call it, 'free.'"

Several of the teens expressed the opinion that music does not precipitate negative behavior, but does reinforce it. In Tonya's words, "I think that music can continue [problem behavior], but I don't think it influences it . . . . Some music can give you evil feelings but it's not going to influence you . . . you've already been influenced to listen to it." Although Tonya isn't a researcher, those "evil feelings" to which she referred appear to be similar to the "aggression-related thoughts and emotions" that were the focus of a recent research study. In fact, a study involving 500 college students contrasted the impact of nonviolent and violent songs. Without regard to differences in musical style or the specific performing artist, violent songs—even humorous ones—increased feelings of hostility without provocation or threat.[12] Needless to say, as aggressive thoughts escalate so do accompanying aggressive behaviors.

* * * * *

No wonder recent research indicates that children who use the most media tend to be the least contented.[13] In order for our children to grow up happy and healthy, it appears that parents must not only be keepers of the remote, the mouse, and the keyboard, but also of the "on" button on the compact disk player.

The following excerpt from a *Time* magazine article gives good insight into why maintaining parental authority in a technology-driven world is difficult to do. "Video games are about letting kids manipulate reality, bend it to their will, which means that when they get up at last from the console, the loss of power is hard to handle. You can't click your little brother out of existence. Plus, no generation has had access to this much information, along with the ability to share it and twist it. Teenagers can . . . invent a new identity [and] escape the boundaries of the household into a very private online world with few guardrails."[14]

Materialism

Why must parents so continuously fight against societal influences? Why do supposedly family-friendly corporations, who turn out millions of toys, video games, movies and music CDs, promote products that obviously do not have children's well-being as top priority? Why are children continually bombarded with advertising that creates an insatiable appetite for things? Let me quote a phrase I've heard my husband use many times in an effort to explain various phenomena: "Just follow the money trail." If you want to attempt to understand what drives individuals, businesses, and societies, determine the financial implications of their actions. Predictably, it seems to be all about money. In light of that, consider the relevance of this Biblical warning written more than 1900 years ago: "The love of money is the root of all kinds of evil."[15]

Society's love affair with affluence and its accompanying power has affected all American families. Those with young children have been hit especially hard by advertising that typifies a greed-over-principle mindset. Here's a case in point. Several years ago, the owner of a large toy-making business won an award for creating a popular line of grotesque and violent toys and comic books. When asked if his own children own the products he created, he is quoted as saying, "Are you kidding? I'm still a dad after five o'clock."[16] Another creator of an extremely violent first-person shooting game with a rating of "mature" openly admits that his goal is to sell it to young children. He's quoted as saying, "It'd be suicide to make the game unplayable by younger people."[17] It occurs to me that "suicide" is an interesting choice of words.

If it seems that marketers know exactly how to entrap your children in the mire of desire and its accompanying whining, you're not experiencing paranoia. One officer for a major market research firm spends her energy rating children's products according to their "nag factor"—their capacity to make children beg. Predictably, companies such as McDonalds, Discovery Zone and Disney work vigorously to get a high rating from her.[18] The fact that children's spending tripled in the 1990s is no fluke. In the battle for our children's loyalty and dollars, successful marketers have a lot to show for their efforts. Incredibly, over $600 billion of household spending, sufficient money to build 1500 major league baseball stadiums, was influenced by children ages twelve and under in the year 2000.[19]

In my opinion, one of the most frightening aspects of this marketing phenomenon is the cult-like zeal of those who have perfected the art. Marketing experts enthuse that a lifetime customer may be worth $100,000 to a retailer, highlighting the financial significance of "cradle to grave" consumer loyalists.[20] The president of Kids-R-Us is quoted as saying that companies "want to own the kids younger and younger."[21] Are marketers succeeding? According to them, at just six months of age, when babies are beginning to say "mama," they are forming mental images of corporate logos and mascots.[22] At three years of age, one out of five American children specifically requests brand-name products.[23] The exploitation of even society's tiniest citizens translates into big bucks for big businesses.

As in every other aspect of parenting, doing what is right for our children in the long term, as opposed to taking the path of least resistance at the moment, is never easy. Much evidence leads us to believe that parents are getting less and less adept at saying "no." Perhaps you recognize the name Carla Wagner, the seventeen-year-old from Coral Gables, Florida who was pegged by local newspapers as the "poster child for spoiled teens."[24] Carla hit and killed a fellow high school student as she was speeding through a suburb in her high-performance Audi A4. Carla, who had spent the afternoon drinking tequila that she charged on her American Express Gold Card, was dialing her cell phone at the time of the accident. The court charged Carla with drunken driving and manslaughter and gave her a trial date. At that point, her parents asked the judge if it was okay if Carla spent the summer in Paris, as usual.[25]

Although Carla may be a classic example of a "spoiled brat," singling her out is a bit unfair. Consider the $20,000 party in Houston for fifty 7-year-olds, who all wore mink coats. Or the Bat Mizvah in New York City where 'N Sync played.[26] According to a CNN/Time poll, two-thirds of parents admit their children are spoiled.[27] And we don't have to look far for supporting evidence. As a call-it-like-it-is reporter reminds us, "Go to the mall or a concert or a restaurant and you can find them in the wild, the kids who have never been told no, whose sense of power and entitlement leaves onlookers breathless, the sand-kicking, foot-stamping, arm-twisting, wheedling, whining despots whose parents presumably deserve the company of the monsters they, after all, created."[28]

Yes, many children are over-indulged and their parents are ultimately responsible. A recent *Newsweek* article refers to "parents who can't say no" as "an unexpected legacy of the 90s."[29]

As discussed earlier, the exploitation of children's

innocence and vulnerabilities by the cleverest marketing minds is just one societal force that has made parenting more difficult with each subsequent generation. There is so much more for children to want, and saying "no" is harder when affluence allows one to say "yes." Additionally, because they are likely to spend more hours at work, parents are eager to do whatever it takes to maintain a relatively conflict-free home atmosphere. Sometimes calming a storm requires a "yes," even when parents know they should say "no."

Another issue related to the problem of materialism is the question of how these children, who are accustomed to getting whatever they desire, will be able to monitor their own spending as they get older. Is there any reason to believe they will somehow become persons characterized by self-control and contentment? A 23-year-old career woman not only provides some insight but validates our concerns.[30] Describing herself as a "recovering spoiled brat" she admits that during her growing-up years she relentlessly manipulated her parents who, in turn, granted her every wish. Once the envy of her friends because she had everything she could possibly want, she now considers it unfortunate that she never learned to live within a budget.

In spite of all of the obvious reasons for concern, I am hopeful the materialistic pendulum is about to begin swinging in the opposite direction. As the phenomenon of excess reaches all-time highs, an increasing number of psychologists, teachers, and parents are realizing that we are doing our children no favors by indulging their every whim. Rather, they believe "it's time to stop the madness and start teaching kids what's really important--values like hard work, delayed gratification, honesty and compassion."[31]

Peers

Directly related to the societal forces just discussed is the power of peer pressure. In our analogy of a journey by sea, peers entering the picture can be likened to buccaneers on board. Although peer influence is certainly not necessarily negative, the reality is that family dynamics invariably change as additional relationships are added to the parent-child mix.

If your children are very young, you aren't yet dealing with the ramifications of their having friends other than those you have chosen. But now is the time to begin thinking about what to expect so you can be proactive, rather than reactive, in dealing with this potentially powerful force in your children's lives. Well before they become teens, most children begin to get their cues on how to talk, act and look from their peers. Although the change is somewhat gradual, this apparent shift of allegiance from parent to peer seems to catch many parents off-guard.

Very rare is the twelve- or thirteen-year-old who does not gravitate toward peers, seeing their approval and acceptance as infinitely more important than that of their parents. Of course, peer pressure is not inherently bad. Just as our children's friends can influence them in a negative sense, they can also do so in a positive sense. Friends who share our values, beliefs, and standards provide a very powerful protective factor for our children.

We all know that regardless of what we say or do, there are no guarantees that our children will not hang out with the "wrong crowd," any more than we can promise our best friend that our toddler will never again bite her toddler. But we *can* be sure that following certain parenting principles will reduce the likelihood that our children will make poor choices when it comes to the selection of friends. As discussed earlier, an over-arching protective factor is one of family connectedness, characterized by mutual unconditional caring and respect. Additionally, loving but firm discipline and monitoring help our children to make wise choices about the friends they choose. We can also affect our children's peer selection in a more direct manner.

When our children are young, we have a great deal of control over when, where, how and with whom they spend their time. By choosing to expose them to particular persons and environments, we are providing our children with early experiences that form the basis of future relationships. For example, when we take our children to church every week, they become friends with others whose families are likely to share our beliefs and values. Our impressionable young children are dependent on us to give direction and make wise choices regarding their peer selection. This, of course, changes over time. Consider the contrast of parental input regarding birthday party guests when our children are four, eight and twelve.

One of the most important ways we can influence our children's friendships is by the behavior we model. Hosting a toddler play group and backyard picnics with other families lets our children know that friends are important and our home is a place where they are welcomed. Although this may not be feasible for every family, we had a standing policy in our home: our children's friends were always welcome. We took the welcome mat on the front porch literally and wanted our children's friends to do so as well.

As our children get older and our influence lessens in terms of their choice of friends, what principles do we want them to have learned from us? Beyond setting the pattern and expectation that their friends spend time in our home, we need to be continually vigilant for opportunities to help them recognize both positive and not-so-positive traits in others. This means that we are not only attempting to instill virtues such as kindness, goodness, and self-control in our own children, but we are also teaching them to assess and appreciate these qualities in others.

Even if we wanted, there is no way we could insulate our children from all external influences. Children enrolled in private and public schools are assigned to classrooms based on their ages; thus, peer groups naturally form. Outside the classroom, the vast majority of extra-curricular activities and youth organizations are organized around their ages.[32] Gradually, children begin to spend more and more time away from adult supervision. By the time they are high school age, they are with their peers more than twice as much as they are with parents or other adults.[33] Rather than trying to protect our children from any and all external influences, we must help them learn to make wise choices on their own.

* * * * *

As we end our discussion on societal influences, do we really believe that the plethora of media offerings in today's world has the potential of greatly harming our children? Are we willing to unplug our children, literally and figuratively, from the bombardment of messages from persons whose values differ greatly from our own? Is it possible that our children will "buy into" the notion that the possession of things translates into happiness? Do we stand ready to encourage our children's association with positive peers? Assuming the answer to each of these questions is yes, we have ample motivation to rise to the level of authority figures with the fortitude to do what is best, not what is easiest, on behalf of our children.

Eleven
THE LIGHTHOUSE

He that will learn to pray, let him go to sea.

- *George Herber[1]*

Recently I heard a bluegrass band sing an old Gospel song. One refrain from the song particularly struck me: "If it weren't for the Lighthouse, where would this ship be?"[2] Because I've already said it's a Gospel song, you probably don't need to be told that the Lighthouse refers to God. Often since I began writing this book I've thought back to the title I'd chosen and envisioned a tiny boat, surrounded by a huge expanse of water, looking a bit adrift and maybe even forlorn, assuming a boat could look that way. How heartening to add to that visual an utterly dependable Lighthouse off on the horizon, whose sole purpose is to guide that small and seemingly insignificant boat safely to its destination.

The Lighthouse not only guides us on a daily basis, He also provides lifelines for us when we're none too sure our boat is going to stay afloat. The lifelines that I will address here are ones that I have found particularly meaningful in my own parenting journey: faith, prayer, the Bible and people. I will begin with faith as it seems to be foundational; without faith there's really no point in reading the Bible or praying.

Although this chapter is written with an emphasis on the importance of a spiritual Presence in our lives, I encourage those of you who don't necessarily agree with that premise to read on. Hopefully you will glean something meaningful and gain appreciation for the depths of direction, reassurance, and strength available to those whose faith is centered in an omnipotent Being.

Faith

Faith allows us, in a time of need, to rely on Someone other than ourselves or any other mere mortal. Take, for instance, the story of the Israelites who found themselves in exile, wandering aimlessly. How reassuring it must have been for them to hear their Father God declaring, "I know the plans I have for you . . . plans to prosper you and not to harm you, plans to give you hope and a future."[3] Through faith, we can claim this promise for ourselves, our spouses and our children. Even when our daily lives and our concept of an ideal family seem to bear no resemblance to each other, the same God who reassured the Israelites also has plans "to prosper and not to harm" our families. If this is true, perhaps you wonder why bad things happen to good people. So do I. Rather than delve into a theological discussion regarding the sovereignty and purposes of God, for which I'm totally unqualified, I'll simply say that when circumstances and events don't make sense, faith enters. Faith allows us to cling to the promise that God always has our good in mind, regardless of how things look from our very limited, human perspective. This explanation is consistent with the Bible's definition of faith: ". . . being sure of what we hope for and certain of what we do not see."[4]

Faith in God also means acknowledging that He knows— even better than we—what's best for our children. Even though many of us would accept this from an intellectual or theoretical perspective, practically we might find it very hard to believe. When one of our sons was going through a particularly rough time I just wanted God to rescue him! After all, God *is* God, which means He can do anything. My prayers were laden with suggestions regarding how God could fix the problem. Then, through the words of a worship song, God spoke to me in a very forceful way.

> It's all about You, Jesus, And all this is for You
> For Your glory and Your fame
> It's not about me, As if You should do things my way
> You alone are God and I surrender to Your ways.[5]

"You alone are God and I surrender to Your ways." Easier said than done! I had to repeat this phrase over and over and over until I was, at least in a small way, ready to "let go and let God." When it comes to our children, surrendering our hopes and dreams is incredibly difficult.

The Bible

Reliance on the Bible and faith are inseparable, for it's only by faith we can claim the literally thousands of promises it contains. Replete with words and imageries to encourage, support and assist us, the Bible is a resource that most of us tap much too infrequently. Its relevance and applicability seem to become particularly apparent when we feel the most anxious or inadequate. In addition to the verses mentioned previously in this book, let me share just a few that served as lifelines in my parenting journey.

When emotional and physical exhaustion take their toll:

- *But those that hope in the Lord will renew their strength, they will soar on wings like eagles; they will run and not grow weary, they will walk and not faint.*[6]

When nothing's making sense and disappointment and disillusionment begin to set in:

- *"For my thoughts are not your thoughts, neither are your ways my ways," declares the Lord. "As the heavens are higher than the earth, so are my ways higher than your ways and my thoughts than your thoughts."*[7]

When my soul is anything but peaceful:

- *You will keep in perfect peace him whose mind is steadfast, because he trusts in you.*[8]

When I'm worried about what might happen today:

- *Don't fret or worry. Instead of worrying, pray . . . . Shape your worries into prayers, letting God know your concerns.*[9]

When I'm worried about what might happen tomorrow:

- *Give your entire attention to what God is doing right now, and don't get worked up about what may or may not happen tomorrow. God will help you deal with whatever hard things come up when the time comes.*[10]

When I lose sight of the significance of my parenting role:

- *The disciples shooed them off. But Jesus was irate and let them know it: "Don't push these children away. Don't ever get between them and me. These children are at the very center of life in the kingdom."*[11]

When my faith is waning:

- *Nothing, you see, is impossible with God.*[12]

When my confidence is shaken:

- *I will praise the Lord, who counsels me; even at night my heart instructs me. I have set the Lord always before me. Because he is at my right hand, I will not be shaken.*[13]

When I wonder if God really cares about me and my family:

- *Are not five sparrows sold for two pennies? Yet not one of them is forgotten by God. Indeed, the very hairs of your head are all numbered. Don't be afraid; you are worth more than many sparrows.*[14]

When I feel the need to fix things myself:

- *...in quietness and trust is your strength.*[15]

When I question whether peace-making is worth the

effort:

- *If it is possible, as far as it depends on you, live at peace with everyone.*[16]

When frustration or anger seem to be taking over:

- *Fathers, don't exasperate your children by coming down hard on them. Take them by the hand and lead them in the way of the Master.*[17]

When I need a reminder of what my children should be seeing in me:

- *So, chosen by God for this new life of love, dress in the wardrobe God picked out for you: compassion, kindness, humility, quiet strength, discipline.*[18]

Prayer

Although we previously talked about praying for and with our children, I am defining "lifeline prayers" as those that we utter when it seems like we and/or our children are facing imminent danger. As I look back over the years that my husband and I have been parents, there were several instances when I had a sense of despair—wracked with fear that something terrible was going to happen to our child. As an infant one of our sons was hospitalized, and we helplessly stood by watching the nurse tie him down with strips of green fabric and prick his tiny arm to begin intravenous feeding. He looked at us pleadingly and screamed for us to rescue him but we could do nothing.

Nothing, that is, but leave him and his future in the loving care of the One who had given him to us in the first place.

The example of our son's illness is likely one to which most parents relate, at least to some degree. But none of us are naïve enough to think that our children's health will be our only, or even necessarily our greatest, concern. Any seasoned parent will tell you that there are countless "opportunities" for distress, such as a toddler who bites, a first grader who can't read, a 10-year-old with no friends, or a 13-year-old who will do whatever it takes to be accepted by peers. Regardless of the situation, lifeline prayers shift the burden from our shoulders to those of an Omnipotent Being. Whew!

The book of Psalms records hundreds of David's lifeline prayers that serve as a model for us. Frequently David simply poured out his heart to God, both when he sensed his helplessness to face his circumstances and when he became overcome by God's goodness to him. I will share a few of David's prayers that are particularly meaningful to me. I encourage you to dig through Psalms (and elsewhere) to find lifeline prayers that suit your own deepest needs.

- *"How long must I wrestle with my thoughts and every day have sorrow in my heart? Look on me and answer, O Lord my God."*[19]
- *"Have mercy on me, O God, have mercy on me, for in You my soul takes refuge. I will take refuge in the shadow of Your wings..."*[20]
- *"When I am afraid, I will trust in You."*[21]

- *Show me Your ways, O Lord, teach me Your paths; guide me in Your truth and teach me, for You are God my Savior, and my hope is in You all day long.*[22]
- *When I said, "My foot is slipping," Your love, O Lord, supported me. When anxiety was great within me, Your consolation brought joy to my soul.* [23]
- *I sought the Lord, and He answered me; He delivered me from all my fears.*[24]
- *I will exalt You, O Lord, for You lifted me out of the depths.*[25]
- *You are awesome, O God...*[26]

Others

So, does this emphasis on faith mean that, assuming we have enough of it, we can sit piously in a corner, read our Bibles, and pray—and be assured that everything will be just fine? Of course not. Having those in our lives with whom we can share our greatest joys and deepest concerns is an invaluable lifeline when fog obscures our path or angry waves threaten to pull us under.

Seeking counsel and comfort requires that we admit (to ourselves and others) that everything is not perfect in our little world. With so much of our own self-worth tied up in whom our children become, vulnerability is painful. But we were not made to live in isolation. True friends who share our values and hopes, and understand our struggles, won't provide hollow reassurances or trite answers. But they will lend much-needed objectivity, perspective and hope.

* * * * *

As we head toward the gleam of the lighthouse, a stubborn faith, relentless prayer, the promises of the Bible and a network of supportive friends serve to reassure us that perhaps the boat isn't quite so small or the sea so wide as it appears to us at the moment.

Twelve
ENJOYING THE JOURNEY

One hundred years from now it will not matter what kind of car I drove, what kind of house I lived in, how much money I had in my bank account, nor what my clothes looked like. But one hundred years from now, the world may be a little better because I was important in the life of a child.

- Author Unknown -

As we come to the end of this brief book, my hope is that you are feeling encouraged and energized. Perhaps some of the principles presented in the previous pages reinforced your philosophy of parenting—yes, you do have a philosophy, even if you've never thought of it as such—and your resolve to give this complex and potentially trying task your very best shot. Perhaps you've decided to make some changes in the way you parent; if so, I trust you are motivated by optimism rather than guilt. Regardless, my prayer is that you close this book convinced of how important you are in the life of your children and, possibly, many other children as well.

Now let me end with a word of caution. As much as I've encouraged you to pour yourself into these parenting years, I want also to urge you to enjoy the journey along the way. Many vacationers choose the quickest mode of getting from point A to point B and look at their destination as the point in time at which the fun begins. Old fashioned road trips have given way to bustling airports, jet-lagged travelers and diminutive packages of pretzels. Of course, efficiency is often a major consideration because the one thing we never seem to have enough of is time. But, in this hurry-up world, the joy of the journey itself seems to be too frequently sacrificed on the altar of expediency. So it can be with parenting.

Yes, parenting is a mammoth task. Yes, we are our children's providers, advocates, protectors and primary source of esteem and identity. Yes, today's parenting decisions need to be governed by long-term plans and goals. Yes, it's a scary world out there. But to see parenting as an overwhelming 24/7 responsibility, with only a very occasional carefree moment, is to risk missing innumerable joys and memorable moments. My final thoughts and suggestions pertain to what I refer to as parenting with a balanced perspective, which allows us to take pleasure in the blessings and appreciate the advances.

Having set the course of your family's journey, relax and take a day at a time rather than living under a veil of concerns for your children's future. Remember to pick some daisies and smell some roses. And keep your sense of humor. I'm not sure of its origin, but a little expression that has helped me attempt to keep life's relatively insignificant incidents in perspective is

"Some day we'll look back and laugh; so why not laugh now?"

Remember that the little hassles of parenting young children are just that: little hassles. Several months ago, I was checking infants and toddlers into our church nursery so their mothers could attend a weekly two-hour parenting study and discussion group. Nine o'clock in the morning can seem quite early to young mothers. Some arrived a few minutes early, some on time, and most arrived after the scheduled beginning time. One was quite late; she came at 9:45 with her two little girls, a 5-month-old in a carrier and an 18-month-old toddler hanging on to her momma's coat tail. The mother's body language and facial expressions indicated it had been a rough morning. The little ones were soon situated in their respective rooms and their mother was writing instructions for the caregivers. When she looked up, she had big tears in her eyes. With a sigh, she said, simply, "It seems like I'll never, ever get anywhere on time." My response was just as simple: "I know it seems that way right now. Let me give you a hug." Such a simple gesture of understanding and caring seemed to rejuvenate her, at least for the moment.

This young mother's frustration should in no way be trivialized. She needs assurance that being late isn't a reflection on the quality of her parenting. Maybe other mothers could get to church on time but, no matter how hard she tried, it seemed that she couldn't. No need to add feelings of inadequacy to the emotions with which she is dealing. (As a postscript to this story, after I wrote this paragraph, I learned that an ultrasound revealed this young mother is expecting twins this spring. I suspect she's going to need a few more hugs, along with lots of casseroles and Pampers.)

Attempt to keep a balanced perspective. No parents or children, even "the best," are perfect. Don't put unrealistic expectations on yourself or on them. Years ago there was a commercial on television promoting a particular brand of children's shampoo. Here's a mother's testimonial: "The shampoo went into his eyes and he cried. I felt like a failure." If shampoo in her son's eyes causes her to feel like a failure, this mother has quite a rough road ahead.

Take time for yourself, to renew and refresh your energy, enthusiasm and outlook. Don't become so wrapped up in your parenting role that you lose your own sense of self. Research repeatedly indicates what we would assume: the empty nest syndrome is very difficult for parents who, for the past 20 years, have used the quality and/or quantity of their parenting to gauge their own self-worth. Remember, "Kids with parents who have a life learn both that they aren't the center of the universe and that they can be free to pursue their own dreams."[1] Maintaining your sense of self is not just good for you; it's good for your children as well.

Never forget that you are engaged in one of the most important vocations in the world: raising your children! You have plenty of years ahead to live in a spotless house, cook a gourmet meal, and enjoy a leisurely lunch with friends. Although teaching a child to say "please" and putting Spiderman bandages on skinned knees draw little attention or acclaim, the long-term significance may be greater than a multi-million dollar corporate deal closed by a CEO in an over-stuffed leather chair in some palatial office. Do you really believe this? I do.

Remember that a sense of efficiency or accomplishment can be difficult to achieve as a full-time, stay-at-home parent. Although a small percentage of fathers assume this role, for the most part it is mothers that grapple with this phenomenon. I strongly advise against asking a stay-at-home mom what she does all day. One reason she dislikes that question so much is because it's so difficult to answer. Some days there's very little tangible evidence, if any at all, to show for one's effort and exhaustion. In terms of household chores, you did two batches of laundry, cleaned part of the house, and eventually fed everyone who was hungry. So what's the state of the household at bedtime? There's dirty laundry heaped on the washing machine, muddy footprints all the way from the back door to the guest bath, and dirty dishes piled high in the sink and spilling over onto the counter. Remind yourself that even if your day's urgent list has few items checked off, the important stuff got done. You wiped noses, picked a bouquet of weeds, read your child's favorite storybook five times, attempted to explain where God lives and kissed away tears. Now go peek in on your bear-hugging toddler in her pink princess sleeper and realize that this picture of absolute innocence and contentment reflects a parent's job well done. Savor the moment.

An unknown author has captured the essence and awe of childhood. "Believe in children. There is faith in their eyes, love in their touch, kindness in their gestures. Thrill with them at life's big and small moments. Hold them close." Rather than continually attempting to disseminate wisdom to our children, we should also be listening, observing and drinking in the freshness of their insights and outlooks. Some of the greatest lessons of life can be learned from, rather than taught to, children. Much can be gained by following children's example of simple trust, unhurried pace, pleasure in little things and forgiving spirits.

Know that the best parents in the world can't shield their children from every bump along the way. Nor should they. When our children were young, a dear friend said something to me that has come to mind hundreds of times through the years: "We aren't growing hot house tomatoes." This little phrase helped me tremendously as I attempted to come to grips with the fact that some of life's storms, from which I desperately wanted to shelter my children, were exactly what they needed to become strong.

Perhaps the ultimate in perspective-taking is to attempt

to grasp how quickly little children grow up. When young children demand nearly 24/7 attention and their needs seem to totally eclipse ours, we feel that we will never have the luxury of coming up for air. But children do grow up—and one of the most common comments of persons with grown children is how quickly the years flew by.

Recently I was asked to introduce the topic of parenting in a newly-formed Sunday School elective for young parents at our church. Late on a Saturday night, here's the way my words spilled out:

You are the most beautiful baby in the whole wide world. I knew you would be.

Can you see me?! I'm mom. YOUR mom. As soon as you can talk, you'll call me Mommy. I'll be the one crying at your wedding.

However, these first few months you'll do most of the crying. My job is to try to figure out why and make it better. I don't like to see you cry.

I'll be your 24/7 personal attendant. If you need anything, don't hesitate to let me know.

Now, we're both very tired tonight. Let's make a deal. I'll sleep past 2:00 a.m. if you will.

I'm so sorry you have to get a vaccination today. I can't stand to see those big tears rolling down your little cheeks.

How adorable. You found your thumb. Gotta get this in your baby book—"sucked thumb for the first time..."

Puh-leeze stop spitting your rice cereal in my face. I've already had my breakfast—this is yours.

Whew, you're getting kinda heavy to lug around. I can't wait until you can walk.

No, no, that's pudding, not finger paint.

Oh, you are the cutest thing. I'm going to call Grandma and tell her that you figured out how to stick out your tongue.

Wow, your first steps—by yourself. You are walking by yourself— already!

This is the last time I'm digging Ernie out of the toilet bowl.

Oh, you bumped your head. That must hurt. I'm sorry.

How, pray tell, did you manage to fit that whole thing in your ear? I wonder if our insurance will cover another visit to the emergency room.

I can't wait until you are old enough to go to preschool. I think you need a little more interaction with peers—and a little less with me.

Stop pulling your sister's hair.

What did you learn about Jesus in Sunday School today?

That's Tommy's truck. Don't take the truck away from Tommy. Hey, Tommy, would you like to play with this cool car instead of that truck?

Are you already old enough to go to kindergarten?

So, you finger painted today, I see. Looks like the teacher must have gotten a good buy on blue paint—lots of blue paint.

Okay, that's it. Time out. And don't come back until you're ready to say you're sorry.

Look, you made your bed all by yourself. You are so grown up!

Hurry and get dressed or you'll be late for your T-ball game.

Wow, you're getting very good at the piano. A couple more lessons and you'll be able to play "Twinkle, Twinkle Little Star" perfectly.

So, is that kid still bothering you at school? Yes? And that's why you don't want to go back again?

I told you that you couldn't go to the birthday party if you didn't clean your room. I know, it's tough. But crying isn't going to help.

Did you make this Mother's Day card all by yourself? It's beautiful. I'm going to put it on the refrigerator where everybody can see it.

Who do you think I am, your 24/7 personal attendant? When are you going to learn to do things for yourself?

Mrs. Johnson called to say she can't find her newspaper. Are you sure you put it on her porch?

I know you hate math homework but you have no choice.

Are you sure you want to play on the Junior High football team? That's a dangerous sport, you know.

I feel like a glorified cab driver. It'll sure be nice when you can drive yourself places.

Were any of your friends at youth group tonight?

You'd better find someone to marry who likes to clean up after slobs.

Are you completely packed for camp? Can't believe you'll be gone two whole weeks.

That's it, you're grounded.

The romance is over? I'm so sorry. I know—you feel like your heart is going to break in two. There's nothing wrong with tears.

Okay, try parallel parking once more. And I'll see if I can keep my eyes open this time.

Absolutely not. Just because all your friends are going to see that trashy movie, doesn't mean you should go.

You'd better get those college applications finished.

The choir concert was wonderful. You didn't tell me you had a solo.

Oh, didn't I tell you that your dad and I are chaperoning the Senior Prom?

I know you're ready to be out on your own. I'm ready too.

Dad and I will head back home just as soon as we get you settled into your new dorm room.

Don't forget to pay your electricity bill. They'll shut your lights off if you forget.

You made the Dean's list! We're so proud of you.

You won't be coming home for Thanksgiving this year? What about Christmas?

Congratulations! I'm happy for you. Yes, I'm crying. They're tears of joy.

Go ahead and take your bedroom furniture. We won't be needing it.

I know you'll only be a 4-hour plane trip away. We'll come when we can.

You know how to reach me 24/7. If you need anything, don't hesitate to let me know.

* * * * *

You are the most beautiful baby in the whole wide world. I knew you would be.

Can you see me?! I'm grandma. YOUR grandma. As soon as you can talk, you'll call me nanna. I'll be the one crying at your wedding.

* * * * *

From baby bottles to soccer balls to wedding bells, seemingly overnight. Most parents with grown children are struck by how quickly the years have flown by. Although some days—or even hours—may seem agonizingly long to you now, I encourage you to enjoy the journey. Before you realize what's happened, *you* will be the one looking back and wondering where time has gone.

Epilogue

God will help a seaman in a storm
but the pilot must still remain at the wheel.

- German Proverb -

I wrote the first chapters of this book several months ago as I was sitting on a sandy beach overlooking the beautiful Gulf of Mexico. And now, as I write these final words, once again I'm looking out over the white sand and rolling waves. As I sit in reverent awe, I contemplate a God who created the deep waters and the creatures within, a God who knows the number of the grains of sand on the shores, a God whose voice the winds and the waves obey. In stark contrast, I think of my own relative insignificance and, yet, how much He cares for all of His creation, including you and me.

Yesterday the sea was calm and the sun shone brightly overhead. I enjoyed the serenity of walking on the beach, dipping my bare feet into the water, and watching children's imaginations being transformed into majestic sand castles. Today, by contrast, the skies are dark, the wind is howling, and the huge waves appear angry as they relentlessly lap at the shore, shaping and reshaping the water's edge. Yesterday a small boat could have sailed peacefully; today, the same boat would be mercilessly tossed about.

So it is with your life—and mine. On some days the air is foggy, the waters choppy, and there's dissension among the crew. On others, the skies are clear and the waters calm.

How are you today? Does your boat seem small in contrast to the wide sea on which you are sailing? Is your compass intact or do you sense it can't be trusted? Have you successfully navigated a storm but fear another just beyond the bend? Do you wonder if your lifeboat is adequate? Can you catch a glimpse of the lighthouse or do you feel quite lost and directionless?

As you continue on your journey, my prayer is that you will be confident as you take the helm, prepared as you navigate the predictable, and buoyant as you sail toward the unknown waters that lie ahead.

References

Chapter 2
[1] Galinsky, E. 1981. *Between generations: The six stages of parenthood*. New York: New York Times Books.
[2] *The Bible*. Isa 40:31 (NIV).
[3] Ibid. James 1:5 (NIV).

Chapter 3
[1] Warren, R. 2002. *The purpose-driven life*. Grand Rapids, MI: Zondervan.
[2] *The Bible*. Luke 2:52 (NIV).
[3] Francis of Assisi. 1181-1226. Founder of Franciscan Order.
[4] *The Bible*. Eph 5:1 (NIV).
[5] Ibid. Deut 6:6 (NIV).
[6] Ibid. Deut 6:7-9 (NIV).
[7] Ibid. Josh 24:14a. (NIV).
[8] Ibid. Josh 24:15a. (NIV).
[9] Ibid. Josh 24:15c. (NIV).
[10] Harris, J. 1995. Where is the child's environment? A group socialization theory of development. *Psychological Review* 102 (3): 458-489.
[11] Gladwell, M. 1998. Annals of behavior. Do parents matter? *The New Yorker*, August 17.

Chapter 4
[1] Plato. 360 BC. *The Republic*. 82.
[2] Brooks, J. B. 2004. *The process of parenting*. Mountain View, CA: Mayfield Publishing Company.
[3] Bailey, B. 2000. *Conscious discipline. 7 basic skills for brain smart classroom management*. Oviedo, FL: Loving Guidance.
[4] Ibid.
[5] Ibid.
[6] Self-Control. 1977. *Music machine: Fruit of the spirit CD*. Sparrow Records.

Chapter 5

[1] Terence. 185–159 BC. Roman Comic Poet.

[2] Brendgen, M., Fran, V., and W. M. Bukowski. 1998. Affiliation with delinquent friends: Contributions of parents, self-esteem, delinquent behavior, and rejection by peers. *Journal of Early Adolescence* 18 (3): 244-265.

[3] Resnick, M. D., Bearman, P. S., Blum, R. W., Bauman, K. E., Harris, K. M., Jones, J., Tabor, J., Beuhring, T., Sieving, R. E., Shew, M., Ireland, M., Bearinger, L. H. and J. R. Udry. 1997. Protecting adolescents from harm. *Journal of the American Medical Association* 238: 223-232.

[4] Samperi, K. 2002. In *Celebrating mothers: A book of appreciation.* Edited by Glorya Hale and Carol Kelly-Gangi, 17. New York: MetroBooks.

[5] *The Bible.* I Cor 12:30b (KJV).

[6] *The Bible.* 13:4 (NIV).

[7] Ibid. 13:7 (NIV).

[8] Garbarino, J. and C. Berdard. 2001. *Parents under siege.* New York: The Free Press. 39.

[9] Reeves, E. J. 1933- . College President (Retired).

[10] Chapman, G. 1996. *The five love languages.* Chicago, IL: Moody Publishers.

[11] Garbarino and Berdard. *Parents under siege.* 126.

Chapter 6

[1] Drucker, P. F. 1909- . Author.

[2] Rainer, T. S. 1997. *The bridger generation.* Nashville, TN: Broadman and Holman.

[3] *The Bible.* James 1:19a (NIV).

[4] Carlson, R. 1998. *Don't sweat the small stuff with your family.* New York: Hyperion. 20.

[5] Tillich, P. 1886-1965. American Theologian.

[6] *The Bible.* Luke 10:40, 41 (NIV).

[7] Ibid. James 1:19a (NIV).

[8] Ibid. James 1:19b (NIV).

[9] Ibid. James 3:9-10 (NIV).

[10] Ibid. James 3:11 (NIV).

[11] Carmichael, A. Date unknown. *If.* London: S.P.C.K., Holy Trinity Church. 37.

[12] *The Bible.* I Cor 13:11 (NIV).

[13]Gordon, T. 1975. *Parent effectiveness training: The tested way to raise responsible children.* New York: Littleton Brown & Co.

[14]*The Bible.* Matt 12:34b (KJV).

Chapter 7

[1] von Goethe, J. W. 1749-1832. German Playwright.

[2] Edward VIII, Duke of Windsor. 1894-1972.

[3] Cloud, Henry and John Townsend. 1998. *Boundaries with kids.* Grand Rapids, MI: Zondervan. 19.

[4] *The Bible.* Eph 6:1 (NIV).

[5] Merriam-Webster Online. 2005. www.m-w.com.

[6] *Parenting without pressure.* www.parentingwithoutpressure.com/ effective_discipline.htm.

[7] Merriam-Webster Online.

[8] Kingsley, Charles. 1819-1875. English Novelist and Poet.

[9] Baumrind, D. 1991. The influence of parenting style on adolescent competence and substance use. *Journal of Early Adolescence* 11 (1): 56-95.

[10]Maccoby, E. E. and J. A. Martin. 1983. Socialization in the context of the family: Parent-child interaction. In *Handbook of child psychology: Socialization personality, and social development.* Edited by P. H. Mussen and E. M. Hetherington, 1-101. New York: Wiley.

[11]Fuligni, A. J. and J. S. Eccles. 1993. Perceived parent-child relationships and early adolescents' orientation toward peers. *Developmental Psychology* 29 (4): 622-632.

[12]Muzi, M. J. 2000. *The experience of parenting.* Upper Saddle River, NJ: Prentice-Hall, Inc.

[13]Steinberg, L. 2005. *Adolescence* (7th Ed.). Boston: McGraw-Hill.

[14]Lamborn, S. D., Mounts, N. S., Steinberg, L. and S, M. Dornbusch. 1991. Patterns of competence and adjustment among adolescents from authoritative, authoritarian, indulgent, and neglectful families. *Child Development* 62:1049-1065.

[15]Shucksmith, J., Glendinning, A., and L. Hendry. 1997. Adolescent drinking behavior and the role of family life: A Scottish perspective. *Journal of Adolescence* 20: 85-101.

[16]Lamborn et al. Patterns of competence and adjustment.

[17]Barber, B. K. 1996. Parental psychological control: Revisiting a neglected construct. *Child Development* 67: 3296-3319.

[18]Eccles, J. S., Buchanan, C. M., Flanagan, C., Fuligni, A., Midgley, C., and D. Yee. 1991. Control versus autonomy during early adolescence. *Journal of Social Issues* 47 (4): 53-68.

[19]Melby, J. N., Conger, R. D., Conger, K. J., and F, O. Lorenz. 1993. Effects of parental behavior on tobacco use by young male adolescents. *Journal of Marriage and the Family* 55: 439-454.

[20]Peiser, N. C. and P. C. L. Heaven. 1996. Family influences on self-reported delinquency among high school students. *Journal of Adolescence* 19: 557-568.

[21]Shucksmith, Glendinning and Hendry. Adolescent drinking behavior.

[22]Lamborn et al. Patterns of competence and adjustment.

[23]Melby et al. Effects of parental behavior on tobacco use.

[24]Peiser and Heaven. Family influences on self-reported delinquency.

[25]Pilgrim, C., Luo, Q. Urberg, K.A. and X. Fang. 1999. Influence of peers, parents, and individual characteristics on adolescent drug use in two cultures. *Merrill-Palmer Quarterly* 45 (1): 85-107.

[26]Resnick et al. Protecting adolescents from harm.

[27]Weiss, L. H., and J. C. Schwarz. 1996. The relationship between parenting types and older adolescents' personality, academic achievement, adjustment, and substance use. *Child Development* 67: 2101-2114.

[28]Boyes, M. C. and S. G. Allen. 1993. Styles of parent-child interaction and moral reasoning in adolescence. *Merrill-Palmer Quarterly* 39 (4): 551-570.

[29]Steinberg. *Adolescence.*

[30]*The Bible.* II Chron 1:10 (NIV).

[31]Dobson, J. 1987. *Dare To Discipline.* Wheaton, IL: Tyndale.

[32]Dinkmeyer, D., Sr., Gary D. McKay, and D. Dinkmeyer. 2005. *The parent's handbook: Systematic training for effective parenting.* San Luis Obispo, CA: Impact.

[33]Bogenschneider, K., Wu, M., Raffaelli, M. and J. C. Tsay. 1998. Parent influences on adolescent peer orientation and substance use: The interface of parenting practices and values. *Child Development* 69 (6): 1672-88.

[34]Miller, K. S., Forehand, R. and B. A. Kotchick. 1999. Adolescent sexual behavior in two ethnic minority samples: The role of family variables. *Journal of Marriage and the Family* 61: 85-98.

Chapter 8
[1] Calloway, B. Author.

[2] *The Bible.* Prov 22:6 (NIV).

[3] Dobson, J. 2001. *Bringing up boys.* Carol Stream, IL: Tyndale Publishers.
[4] *The Bible.* Ps 78:5-7 (NIV).
[5] Lewis, C.S. 1950-56. *The chronicles of Narnia.* United Kingdom: HarperCollins Publishers.
[6] Patience. 1977. *Music machine: Fruit of the spirit.* Sparrow Records.
[7] Kids under construction. 1995. *Kids Under Construction Audio Cassette Tape.* Word Entertainment Music.
[8] Gannon, Kim and Walter Kent. *Johnny Appleseed grace.*

Chapter 9
[1] van der Post, L. and Taylor, J. 1986, November. Testament to the bushmen. *Reader's Digest.*
[2] *The Bible.* Ps 18:30 (NIV).
[3] Mead, M. 1901-1978. American Anthropologist.
[4] Resnick et al. Protecting adolescents from harm.
[5] *U. S. Bureau of Census, Statistical Abstract of the United States.* (121st Ed.). 2002. Washington, DC: U.S. Government Printing Office.
[6] *Turn around.* 1964. Words and music by Harry Belafonte, Alan Greene and Malvina Reynolds. Artists: Kingston Trio. Album: *Time to Think.*
[7] *The Bible.* I Cor 14:40 (NIV).
[8] *Ibid.* Prov 17:22 (NIV).

Chapter 10
[1] Caleb, C. 1780-1832. British Sportsman Writer.
[2] Annenberg Public Policy Center. *Media in the home 2000: The fifth annual survey of parents and children.* www.appcpenn.org/reports/2000.
[3] *Media Violence in Children's Lives.* A position statement of the National Association for the Education of Young Children. www.naeyc.org/about/positions/pdf/PSMEVI98.PDF.
[4] Ibid.
[5] Ibid.
[6] Centerwall, B. S. 1992. Journal *of the American Medical Association* 267:3059-3063.
[7] American Health Association, American Academy of Pediatrics, American Psychological Association, American Psychiatric Association, American Academy of Family Physicians, and American Academy of Child & Adolescent Psychiatry. 2000, July 26. *Joint statement on the impact of entertainment violence on children.*

[8] Grossman, D. and G. Kloske. 1996. *On killing: The psychological cost of learning to kill in war and society.* New York: Littleton Brown & Co.

[9] American Academy of Pediatrics. 2001, November. Media violence policy statement. *Pediatrics* 5: 1222-1226.

[10] Garbarino and Berdard. *Parents under siege.*

[11] Ibid., 200-201.

[12] Anderson, C.A., Carnagey, N.L., and J. Eubanks. 2003. Exposure to violent media: The effects of songs with violent lyrics on aggressive thoughts and feelings. *Journal of Personality and Social Psychology* 84: 960-971.

[13] Roberts, D. F., Foehr, Ulla G., Rideout, Victoria J., and Mollyann Brodie. 1999, November. *Kids & media @ the new millennium.* www.kff.org/content/1999/1535/KidsReport%20FINAL.pdf.

[14] Gibbs, N. 2001, August 6. Who's in charge here? *Time.* 158:5.

[15] *The Bible.* Timothy 6:10 (NIV).

[16] Kaplan, D. 1997, August 4. Caped crusader. *Newsweek.* Cited in Ruskin, Gary. *Why they whine: How corporations prey on our children.* www.mothering.com/articles/growing_child/consumerism/whine.html.

[17] Gelmis, J. 1999, May 11. Shoot to thrill or shoot to kill? *Newsday.* Cited in Ruskin. *Why they whine.*

[18] *Western initiative media.* Cited in Ruskin. *Why they whine.*

[19] McNeal, J. U. 2001, July 30. Quoted in McDonald, M. Call it 'kid-fluence.' *U.S. News & World Report,* 32.

[20] McNeal, J. and C. Yeh. 1993, June. Born to shop. *American Demographics.* 15.

[21] Ruskin, G. *Why they whine.*

[22] McNeal and Yeh. Born to shop.

[23] Center for a New American Dream. 1999. *New poll shows marketing to kids taking its toll on parents, families.* www.newdream.org/campaign/kids/press-release.html.

[24] Gibbs, N. 2001, August 6. Who's in charge here? *Time* 158:5.

[25] Charles, N., Trischitta, L. and S. Morissey. 2001, August 31. End of the party. *People Weekly.* 56:i7.

[26] Gibbs, Who's in charge here?

[27] Ibid.

[28] Ibid.

[29] Tyre, P., Schelfo, J. and B. Kantrowitz. 2004, September 13. The power of no. *Newsweek.*

[30] Ibid.

[31] Ibid.

[32] Steinberg. *Adolescence.*

[33] Brown, B. 2004. Adolescents relationships with peers. In *Handbook of adolescent psychology.* Edited by R. Lerner and L. Steinberg. New York: Wiley.

Chapter 11

[1] Herbert, G. 1593-1632. British Poet.

[2] *The Lighthouse.* 1991. Words and music by Robbie Hinson.

[3] *The Bible.* Jer 29:11 (NIV).

[4] Ibid. Hebrews 11:1 (NIV).

[5] *Jesus, Lover of My Soul.* ©1995. Kingsway's Thankyou Music. Words and music by Paul Oakley.

[6] *The Bible.* Isa 40:31 (NIV).

[7] Ibid. Isa 55:8, 9 (NIV).

[8] Ibid. Isa 26:3 (NIV).

[9] Ibid. Phil 4:6 (MSG).

[10] Ibid. Matt 6:34 (MSG).

[11] Ibid. Mark 10:14 (MSG).

[12] Ibid. Luke 1:37 (MSG).

[13] Ibid. Ps 16:7,8 (NIV).

[14] Ibid. Luke 12:6,7 (NIV).

[15] Ibid. Isa 30:15b (NIV).

[16] Ibid. Rom 12:18 (NIV).

[17] Ibid. Eph 6:4 (MSG).

[18] Ibid. Col 3:12 (MSG).

[19] Ibid. Ps 13: 2, 3a (NIV).

[20] Ibid. Ps 57:1 (NIV).

[21] Ibid. Ps 56:3 (NIV).

[22] Ibid. Ps 25: 4,5 (NIV).

[23] Ibid. Ps 95:18, 19 (NIV).

[24] Ibid. Ps 34: 4 (NIV).

[25] Ibid. Ps 30:1 (NIV).

[26] Ibid. Ps 68:35a (NIV).